INSURANCE

Auto. Home.
Renters. Business.
Commercial Truck.

TRADELINES

Tradeline Pricing

CREDIT REPAIRS

Credit
Improvement

In Financial Playaz, every issue you'll discover new ways to make more money, and keep more of the money you make.

Financial Playaz is a financial magazine that gives the best advice on how to create a more profitable future for yourself and your loved ones. We seek to help people with their investments, taxes, retirement planning, and other personal finance issues.

Our objective is to educate and give real-world advice and guidance to guarantee a financially secure future. We know making major financial decisions can be tough, and we're here to guide you every step of the way. You will get the best Financial Playaz has to offer on personal finance topics that matter most to you, including:

- Investing and building wealth,
- Reducing your tax burden,
- Planning for a financially secure retirement,
- Making major purchases such as a home, a business or car,
  And much more.

Sheik Trice
editor-in-chief

from the editor

FINANCIAL PLAYAZ

Editor in Chief	Sheik Trice
Creative Director	Lightworkers LLC.
Managing Editor	Andrea Jackson
Featured Interview	Shawn Williams
Entrepreneur Highlight	Ruler
Contributor	Torry T. Davis
Contributor	Jered Sturm
Contributor	Anthony Davis

ONE SOURCE FINANCIAL, INC

**Financial Playaz is a subsidiary of One Source Financial, Inc.
For inquiries or suggestions, contact us at:**

(800) 654-9901
onesourcefinancialinc@gmail.com

P.O. Box 8781
Elkridge, MD 21075

www.onesourcefinancialinc.com

CONTENTS

A MINOR SETBACK FOR A MAJOR COMEBACK

AN INTERVIEW WITH SHEIK TRICE

FP) How long have you been home and how long were you incarcerated?

ST) I have been home since February 4, 2021. COVID sent me home two years early. It's funny because my cell-mate talked me into it.

FP) So what exactly did you have to do for early release?

ST) I had to submit a BP 8 and a BP 9?

FP) What is a BP 8 and BP 9?

ST) Those are Administrative Remedies. The grievance process usually begins by filling out a BP-8 form (also known as an informal complaint or cop-out) and giving it to Staff. The formal complaint process begins by filing a Request for Administrative Remedy (BP-9) and giving it to the Warden. The BP-9 complaint must be filed within 20 calendar days from the date of the incident, unless it was not feasible to do so, which should be documented in the complaint. The Warden has 20 calendar days to respond, which may be extended for an additional 20 calendar days. If the individual does not receive a response, the issue should be considered unresolved and proceeds to the next step. I was at Butner low at the time so I hired someone to write a motion for me, the next thing I know I received a public defender from the courts, and the rest is history.

FP) So what's the name of your company and what services do you provide?

ST) One Source Financial Inc., provides services preparing taxes, credit repair, tradelines, incorporating businesses, insurance (truck, home, rental, car, commercial, & business).

FP) How long have you been in business?

ST) The company was incorporated in 2018 and active in 2019. I wasn't really making money until I came home in February 2021.

FP) Who are your customers?

ST) We have customers from all backgrounds and professions. Just being able to talk to customers who are truck drivers, doctors, lawyers, educators, inmates, about their experience dealing with us helps us out tremendously.

FP) How did you get started and what made you want to get into finance?

ST) I love money so much I wanted a better understanding so I started studying it. I would call home and ask for certain books, surround myself with people that can teach me something I didn't already know. I took the good habits home with me, so the grind doesn't stop. I was preparing myself for the arrival, it was a minor setback for a major comeback. I had good credit in the streets, but not corporate credit. I had to get my credit fixed, so I started working on it while I was incarcerated. Once I got it to where I needed it to be, I applied for credit cards and had my mom and my fiancée use them and keep them in

FP) So you decided to get into finance while you were incarcerated or were you doing this before?

ST) I have been hustling and dealing with finances all my life, now I understand how it all works. It's all about finding passive income so you're making money while you sleep and I started learning all of this while I was in prison. There is a lot of knowledge in the prison system that you can get for free, because you will get charged out here. I'm not a financial guru, but I am hungry for knowledge so I continue to eat.

FP) What is passive income?

ST) Passive income is a source of income that requires minimal effort to achieve. Income from a rental property, investments on the stock market. It's income you can earn without having to physically trade your time for money like you would with an active income you make from a job.

ST) good standing. The banks want to give you money, they just want to make sure you pay them back, you get judged by that 3 digit score.

It's essential that you get your credit score together. They say cash is king, but I disagree. Credit is king. I don't want to use my money. I rather keep mine and use other's people money (OPM). My experience is my expertise, so I started my company to help other people learn about finances and better ways to make money. It started out with just my fiancee and I. Now we are assembling a strong team. It doesn't matter if you're incarcerated or in the free world, we want everyone to eat. A lot of people ask how my business took off so quickly. It's all about positioning yourself. I know this might sound cliche, but it's chess not checkers and I'm striving to win. Every move I make has to be strategic, I can't freestyle it. When you plan and stick with it and move accordingly everything will align with the universe. I incorporated my company while I was incarcerated and didn't know how I was going to run it. I just wanted it up and I would figure out the rest later.

FP) So does your company have clients they trade stocks for?

ST) My company doesn't trade stocks but we are affiliated with companies that do. That's the great thing about having resources. I love networking and surrounding myself around people that can help bring me to the next level.

FP) So what inspired you to want to work with inmates?

ST) I know what it's like to not have any support, so I want to help anyway that I can. I know I'm not going back to prison and there are a lot of people that feel the same way. There are a lot of smart individuals that have the same ambition I have and I figure if we all can come together it will make us stronger.

We have to create our own opportunity and go get it ourselves. I also know a lot of people have money and don't know what or how to go about investing it. So I decided to create a magazine, Financial Playaz, to educate my peers on financial literacy. The inmates are therapeutic for me; they keep everything in perspective. They remind me of the COs talking crazy, the lockdowns, chicken patties on Tuesday's chicken on Thursday's I know what it's like. I'm not trying to go back to eating mackerel patties, so I have to stay focused on what I'm striving to do.

FP) So your fiancee is your business partner, how did that come about?

ST) I met my fiancee, business partner, on this app called Plenty of Fish. One night I'm laying in my bunk and I asked my guy for a zip code. He was from DC so he gave me a Maryland zip code. I posted one picture and my inbox was lit and that's when I saw her picture, that was the first person I called and we hit it off real good. I was talking to other women at the time, but she was knocking them out of the box quickly. She told me

that she was going to ride until the wheels fell off and she's still riding to this day. She's the true definition of a ride or die chick. She was really smart and it helped that she was already in Corporate America. My mother was doing some administrative work for me, but I didn't want to bother her so I kept it at a minimum. When Andrea came into my life, she took the company to another level. Whatever I asked her to do, she would do it and more. I learned a lot from her because she would do a lot of research. She's a go-getter. I call the plays and she executes it, a perfect match. Her becoming my business partner was an easy decision.

FP) So does all of your income come in from your business, or you have other streams of income.

ST) I have money invested in stocks, real-estate and I also do some sports betting. I'm looking to get my own investment property this summer also with a luxury car so I can rent it out on turo and consumers can rent it for their videos. I have a plan, just have to stay focused and stay on the grind. Anything you want you have to work hard for it, nothing coming easy and I wouldn't want it any other way.

FP) I wasn't expecting you to mention gambling, so you're not afraid of losing your money?

ST) Gambling? Everything is a gamble, it's about your risk tolerance. Some people take larger risks than others. Some people park their money in the bank, life insurance policies, real-estate, stocks, mutual funds. You have people that play with options, futures, day trading; these are all risks. I take calculated risks. I diversify my portfolio, I spread it out, when I gamble it's only with 10% of my bank roll. I play it safe. The only money I have in the bank is what I call liquid money, that's to pay bills. I also have an emergency fund, that's also liquid cash. Everything else is invested. Now I'm not doing this with a lot of money but It doesn't matter because my system is in place, it helps me not to fuck my money up. Whether it's 1,000 dollars or a million, the system is in place.

FP) How was the transition from prison to the streets?

ST) This wasn't my first time coming out of prison, so I knew what to expect. Now don't get me wrong, I understand times will get hard, but that's part of life, you just have to be prepared for it.When you check the weather report and it says rain you're prepared for it. That's how life works, you're going to have your peaks and valleys just be mentally prepared because it's coming. Time moves fast so don't waste it because it will pass you by. It was easy for me because I have a support group. I had no money when I walked out the gates, but when I touched Jersey my people hit me with enough bread to keep my head above water. I was also building my credit while incarcerated, that put me ahead of the game. Whoever is reading this needs to know just because you're incarcerated doesn't mean that you can't build your credit. If you can do it now then get it done because that will give you leverage. Apply for a credit card because age on a card is very important and while

you are doing your time the card is getting older. Food for thought: If you're trying to start your own company, do your research and start preparing for it now while you have the time, because you will never have this much time again. Take advantage of the opportunity.

FP) What makes you say it's an opportunity?

ST) I say it's an opportunity because you have enough time to get your shit together, mentally, physically, and spiritually. You have to do the time, so you might as well find opportunity in it.

FP) What do have to say to the men and women behind these walls?

ST) To the soldiers that I left behind, I just want y'all to know that I didn't forget about you, when I got immediate release, I left before my property got to my destination. My phone book never made it home but you can find me at onesourcefinancialinc@gmail.com. If you don't have life you have a date and you will be back out here so just prepare yourself. To all my lifers, don't give up. I know a lot of men that got time back, so keep fighting. Your time will come.

> "If you're trying to start your own company, do your research and start preparing for it now while you have the time, because you will never have this much time again."

HOW MONEY WORKS

By Jered Sturm

The key to mastering anything is understanding the foundation or base of the concept so you can build on it. As investors, our root goal is often to turn money into more money. If that is the case, then isn't it important to understand what money is, where it comes from, and how it works at the base level?

In school, we are not taught about money on a macro or even micro level. Many do not understand the basic concepts of money, let alone how money works. Stepping back and looking at our monetary system as a whole gives us the ability to look at investments with a wider lens than just focusing on a small part of the grand scheme.

Many look at investments by focusing only on the specific asset. This would be like watching a football game through a drinking straw. You might be able to get a clear picture of the ball, but you don't really know what is going on around the ball to make it go up and down the field.

Looking at the asset and the market would be like watching the same football game through a paper towel cardboard tube.

You would see some of the players close to the ball and understand why the ball is moving one way or the other. But if you remove the straw or tube and look through a full, unobstructed perspective, you will see the coaches calling plays, the weather that affects the play calls, the team of coordinators up in the box relaying information down to coaches and players, and many other important factors.

To gain a full perspective of investing look at the whole system — how money works and why all parties are incentivized to do what they are doing. Understanding this will allow you to answer some basic questions like "Why should I invest in real estate?" or help you see opportunities where others miss.

If we want to start at the root of an investment, it is vital to understand what money is, how it works, and what incentives are behind all parties involved in a transaction. To understand this, I believe we have to understand our monetary system. Our monetary system is a complex shell game mixed with smoke and mirrors that are hardly ever discussed, let alone taught. In this article, I will do my best to describe how the United States' and many other countries' monetary system works. I will then share specific examples of how this information can be utilized in real world investing with a focus on real estate.

OUR MONETARY SYSTEM

Our current monetary system in the U.S. starts at the United States Treasury. The Treasury creates a bond to place for sale at a bond auction. A treasury bond essentially is an IOU that states, "If you (buyer) gives me X dollars, I (treasury) will give you Y% interest on that money over Z years, plus the full X dollars in principal."

If the U.S. treasury says, "We would like to sell $1 trillion in bonds," who steps up and buys them? The world's biggest banks do. Then those banks look for buyers of the bonds at a premium. Here is where the Federal Reserve comes in. The Federal Reserve will buy the bonds from the big banks and wire them a nice payday of electronic money. You may wonder where the Fed got all that money from. They created it out of thin air not by printing, but by simply doing an electronic credit to the big banks' account at the Fed.

You may be scratching your head. So, let me break this down: Big Bank X bought a $2 trillion bond and sold it to the Federal Reserve for $2 trillion, plus a premium. The Fed then says, "Instead of me sending you a check, why don't I just credit the savings account you have here at the Fed?" Big Bank X says, "Sure, go ahead." With a couple of keyboard strokes, the Fed just created $2 trillion of electronic currency sitting in Big Bank X's account.

Sounds like nonsense? Here is a quote from our former chairman of the Fed, Ben Bernanke, describing the real world example back in 2012 during a lecture at George Washington University:

"Now, you might ask the question, well, the Fed is going out and buying 2 trillion dollars of securities — how did we pay for that? And the answer is that we paid for those securities by crediting the bank accounts of the people who sold them to us, and those accounts, at the banks, showed up as reserves that the banks would hold with the Fed. So the Fed is a bank for the banks. Banks can hold deposit accounts with the Fed, essentially, and those are called reserve accounts. And so as the purchases of securities occurred, the way we paid for them was basically by increasing the amount of reserves that banks had in their accounts with the Fed."

So now magically Big Bank X has all this money in its account at the Fed. What will Big Bank X do with all this new money in its accounts? Well, Big Bank X just did pretty well in buying treasury bonds, so why not go buy some more? They go back to the bond auction, buy more bonds, and yet again, the Fed buys the bonds by crediting their account. This leaves the Treasury with a bunch of electronic money the bankers paid them. Big Bank X is nice and rich from the premiums. And the Fed is unaffected because all they did was enter a transaction on the computer to make it happen, and now they start collecting the Y% interest on the bonds they own.

If you still are scratching your head thinking, "No they can't do that," here is a quote right from Federal Reserve Bank of Boston, Putting It Simply (1984): "When you or I write a check there must be sufficient funds in our account to cover the check, but when the Federal Reserve writes a check there is no bank deposit on which that check is drawn. When the Federal Reserve writes a check, it is creating money."

But 4 years later, since the magically created $2 trillion has worked its way through our banking system and has become $20 trillion in private debt, the currency supply has magnified, and because of that, the prices on everything have gone up to reflect the excess supply of currency. This increase in prices includes prices on aircraft carriers. So for example if the government buys 100 aircraft carriers for $2 trillion, but now maybe $2 trillion will only buy 90 aircraft carriers because their prices went up along with everything else. This means their 100 aircraft carriers may now be worth $2.2 trillion dollars, but they still only owe the fixed $2 trillion they borrowed. When the dollar is worth less, it makes paying off existing debt easier.

Inflation eating away purchasing power is a tricky thought to grasp, so let's look at another example. Joe buys a brand new house in 1970 for $22,000, which was the median new home price in the United States in 1970. Joe finds a banker that gives him a 30-year fixed rate mortgage.

But wait! Now the treasury has a whole bunch of money. What do they do with it? They spend it! They give it out to different parts of the government, and they spend it on roads, bridges, social programs, and the military.

The owners and employees of the construction companies, government organizations, and any other companies/individuals who make money from these government expenditures then put their paychecks into their bank accounts for safe keeping.

FRACTIONAL RESERVE BANKING

Because we and many other countries use a fractional reserve banking system, banks can now lend a percentage of their total deposits. Although reserve ratios can change, in many cases banks are allowed to lend out 90% of all deposits and keep 10% on reserve for account holders to withdraw if they want their money. This means 90% of the money the workers in our example earned and put into their bank ends up getting lent out. But that money goes somewhere, right? Yes. I'll give a specific example to explain where it goes.

For a specific but very basic example of fractional reserve banking and what it does to our currency supply, we'll look at a school teacher. Let's say a teacher makes $50,000 and has it directly deposited into her bank account. The bank then can and does lend out $45,000, or 90%, of her deposits. Let's say that the bank decides to lend $45,000 to a company to buy a work truck. The truck dealer who sold the truck then takes the $45,000 payment and deposits it into their bank account. The bank then lends out 90% of that, or $40,500, to someone who wants a boat. The buyer of the boat then hands $40,500 to the seller, and the boat seller deposits it into his/her account. And then the boat seller's bank lends out 90%. This goes on and on until the $50,000 that the teacher deposited is expanded to $500,000 in bank loans.

When you hear that there isn't any money being printed, they are not lying. The printers might not be running, but the currency is being stretched through our banking system. The reality is 92%-96% of all currency created is

formed in this exact banking system. This constant increase in currency in the economy is sure to have an effect. The more currency in the cycle, the higher prices climb to meet that supply of currency. Everyday people then work to pay for those items that now cost more. We all trade our life and our time here on Earth in exchange for money to buy those very things that keep increasing in cost.

When the Dollar is Worth Less, it Makes Paying Off Existing Debt Easier.

What does this all mean? This means the U.S. Treasury is taking on trillions and trillions of debt — roughly $19.5 trillion when I wrote this article, but you can see the real time debt figure here. They are doing this by borrowing dollars into creation from the Fed, which increases the currency supply and inevitably causes inflation.

Why would the treasury want inflation? It makes the massive debt figure hurt less and easier to pay. Let me explain. Four years ago in our example, the treasury borrowed $2 trillion. That $2 trillion maybe had a purchasing power able to purchase 100 aircraft carriers for our military.

But 4 years later, since the magically created $2 trillion has worked its way through our banking system and has become $20 trillion in private debt, the currency supply has magnified, and because of that, the prices on everything have gone up to reflect the excess supply of currency. This increase in prices includes prices on aircraft carriers. So the government got to buy 100 aircraft carriers for $2 trillion, but now maybe $2 trillion will only buy 90 aircraft carriers because their prices went up with everything else. This means their 100 aircraft carriers may now be worth $2.2 trillion dollars, but they still only owe the fixed $2 trillion they borrowed. When the dollar is worth less, it makes paying off existing debt easier.

Inflation eating away purchasing power is a tricky thought to grasp, so let's look at another example. Joe buys a brand new house in 1970 for $22,000, which was the median new home price in the United States in 1970 (you can find the data at https://dqydj.com/historical-home-prices/). Joe finds a banker that gives him a 30-year fixed rate mortgage. Joe borrows the full $22,000. Over the next 30 years, Joe pays down his mortgage. As he pays down this mortgage, his house, like the price of everything else, slowly climbs due to inflation. But does Joe ever have to pay any more principal than the agreed upon $22,000? No. The debt is a bookmark in time, freezing the dollar's purchasing power in 1970, even though everything else in the world continues to get more expensive.

The government understands this. Their debt is easier to pay as the dollar's purchasing power becomes diluted through inflation. On top of this, the increased inflation helps slide income levels up, pushing individuals into higher tax brackets, which makes it easier to collect more taxes to pay for all that interest on the debt.

If you don't believe me take it straight from the Federal Reserve's mouth:

The decrease in purchasing power incurred by holders of money due to inflation imparts gains to the issuers of money.

— St. Louis Federal Reserve Bank, Review, Nov. 1975, P.22

There is one piece of the puzzle that we haven't covered. Do you remember way back in the beginning when the Fed did some computer entries to buy bonds that pay Y% interest?

Well, that means the Treasury, who issued the bonds, owes the Fed Y% interest plus the principal. That has to come from somewhere. Ah, yes, the IRS will collect that money for the treasury through income taxes. Yep, our hard-earned money that is taxed goes to paying off debt rather than fixing our schools, roads, or anything else useful.

HOW THIS RELATES TO YOU

If you made it this far, you may be thinking, "How in the heck does this relate to me?" It greatly does, and understanding how our money works gives you the ability to see things differently. Not only will it show you how our monetary system is a scam, it will enlighten you to align yourself with the inevitable outcome of this madness.

Why not play the same game as our government? Remember our example of Joe buying his house back in 1970 with debt? Why couldn't we do the same thing with all our investment properties? I have said several times in other articles, "The most powerful tools in real estate are debt and taxes." Debt freezes the dollar's purchasing power in time, and real estate is the most tax-friendly asset class there is.

I can only believe the amount of money falsely created and injected into our economy during the past years of quantitative easing making its way through the banking system will result in inflation. It may take a few years and a few events to happen because much of that money is roosting overseas at this point. But I believe when you increase the amount of currency in the system like our government has, we are bound to see the purchasing power of the dollar go down.

This is why debt is powerful, bookmarking in time the purchasing power prior to seeing the inflationary results of our government's actions. By doing this, you are simply aligning your interest with those in charge.

Ultimately, our monetary system has two paths: It can hyper-inflate, or America will have to make a full-blown overhaul to the monetary system. It is my personal belief that countries will lose faith in the dollar and begin trading in other currencies and dump their U.S. bonds. This will result in much of our quantitative easing money coming back from overseas, and we will go into hyperinflation.

In either scenario, I want to be holding tangible assets like real estate. If prices skyrocket from inflation, good for real estate investors. We will see massive appreciation, increases in rent, and we still only owe our original debt at the lower costs. If the dollar goes down in a blaze and we have a full-blown overhaul, I would like to own something people still need, so that way, whatever the next monetary system comes into play, my assets will be worth lots of the new currency.

Understanding the monetary system can also affect factors in day-to-day operations rather than only macro analysis. Recently, on the purchase of a multimillion dollar apartment complex, I negotiated a 5% increase

in LTV if I deposited the 5% difference in a CD at their bank. Until I made this offer, I was stuck at 75% LTV. Once I made this offer, we bumped to an 80% LTV.

Why would they do this? Because they were able to go lend 90% of my CD out to someone else and earn more interest on it. I was happy because I am going to pull the CD money out in 12 months. But in 12 months, does the bank have to call in the loan they gave out on my CD deposit? Nope. Because I understood how the monetary system worked, I was able to borrow an additional $100k. Which, of course, is a good thing, as that debt will likely be diluted through inflation.

Or how about taking the economic concepts of the monetary system and focusing them on a specific demographic or psychographic group? For example, if minimum wage goes up to $15 an hour, what do you think will happen? Many say, "Well, all the low-income earners will be replaced with robots." Yes, maybe some, but what is shown in countless studies is that more frequently prices of items that are a primary cost to the people of that specific demographic will rise.

> *It's just a matter of fact when it comes to free market economics.*

This is because the currency was forced into one demographic, and in a free market, the prices always adjust for excess currency. The ability to rent (demand) will go up with supply staying stagnant. If the minimum wage gets bumped to $15 an hour, do you think you can expect rental rates in C and D class property to go up? Absolutely. It's not a discussion of if that's morally right or wrong; it's just a matter of fact when it comes to free market economics.

It is so important to understand how our monetary system works and understand why the government does things it does. Having that understanding will allow you the ability to look at investments through a full lens perspective. If you can understand, you can position your own investments in a way that aligns with the interests of those who call the shots, while also protecting yourself if things crash and burn from the madness.

HOW TO GET STARTED IN BUSINESS

With the Great Resignation and people starting businesses in droves, knowing how to start a business is essential information for anyone contemplating going out on their own. People may be drawn to the freedom lifestyle but may not understand how much work is involved.

You need to be aware of what you are getting into when you leave steady employment and income to start your own business. Starting a business is hard work, and if it were easy, everyone would be doing it. It's not uncommon to hear stories of entrepreneurs who ditched their 9-5 only to become involved in their business and work 24/7. It takes much work and a lot of sweat equity to reap the rewards, especially in the beginning.

7 PRO TIPS TO CONSIDER WHEN STARTING A BUSINESS

1. IDENTIFY A NEED

The world is not a perfect place and will never be the perfect place. You can find different unsatisfied needs on the market, different not completely satisfied needs, different unsolved or partially solved problems.

These types of imperfections exist on the market, and that can be a business opportunity for you.

When you see something that you can fix, improve, change, transform, or reinvent, you can translate it into a business opportunity.

So, open your eyes. You don't know from where will come new business opportunities for your company.

2. CREATE MARKET RESEARCH

You will need to do initial market research. What type of products or services do you want to offer? Who are individuals or businesses that will use your products/services? How often will they need to use those products and/or services? What are the benefits of your products and services for your customers? Are there similar or the same products on the market? How will your products or services be different from the competitor's products and services? How will you reach potential customers? What type of marketing weapons will you use to reach potential customers? These are essential questions in this second step of building your business to give you the basics of everything else you will need to do.

3. MAKE A BUSINESS PLAN

The business plan results in a product from your business planning process that will give you concrete action steps you will need to grab an opportunity, monitor your achievements, and of course, improve all your past failures. You will have the answers on how much money you will need, who will be your partners, your responsibilities, who will work for your business, your cash flow, the break-even point, etc.

4. CREATE BUSINESS BUDGET

Knowing how much money you must work with and not overspend is vital to growing your business. Starting a new business is expensive, and the cash outlay is demanding. There are many competing demands for your dollar when starting a business, and you need to be conscientious of your business budget.

5. BRING IN SALES

The most important job you have in your business is to bring in sales. The first thing after you start your business is to sell. But, not only to sell but always to try to sell more and more to your customers. Selling is the most critical function, especially in the early startup stage. You need a client base who know, like and trust you, so focus on creating relationships with potential clients.

6. REINVEST YOUR PROFITS

When you have hit profitable months, it is wise to reinvest that profit to grow your business. Bootstrapping means that as you make money in your business, you can invest in products or services that will help grow your business.

7. DON'T OVERLEVERAGE

Many business owners love to bootstrap their business not to take on debt. To overleverage your business means taking on too much debt. Too much debt is risky in business due to the borrowing costs of that debt. Too much strain on cash flow will close a business down. The bottom line is that there are many ways to start a business but to start a company that will be financially viable and successful, you need to

have business financial literacy skills. Knowing how to build a business that will support you financially is part of the battle, but if you want to create a company that will allow you to grow and develop wealth for yourself, you need to understand how to make that. Considering 82% of businesses fail due to financial mismanagement, knowing how to manage your business finances will increase your success rate.

• • • • • • • • • • • • • • • • • • • •

QUESTION: DO YOU HAVE EXPERIENCE WITH STARTING UP YOUR OWN BUSINESS. CAN YOU SHARE YOUR ENTREPRENEURIAL EXPERIENCE WITH US?

the inter view

with Andrea Jackson

FP) How did One Source Financial Inc. get started?

AJ) I met a guy from prison online. I didn't know that he was in prison nor did he reveal it.

FP) Do you know he was incarcerated?

AJ) I met him on Plenty of Fish (POF). At the time I wasn't in a relationship, so I decided to try something different. I wanted to find someone that was not in my area and my girlfriend told me about POF. When I was looking at the pictures on the app I ran across his picture and found him attractive. So I inboxed him and when he responded we spoke on the phone for hours. We hit it off great.

FP) Is that when you found out he was in prison?

AJ) I didn't find out he was in prison until a week later. I was under the impression he was a free man because the amount of time we spent on the phone. So when he finally told me I was in shock. I never dated someone who was in prison. At that time I really liked him, so I wanted to see what this was about. I remember the first time I went to visit him. He was in a prison in New Jersey called Fort Dix. I was extremely nervous, because our first date was in a prison visiting room and on top of that I ran into my cousin, she was visiting her husband. We thought her husband was in Africa on a business trip, but instead he was in Fort Dix.

Our family can be real bougie, so we decided this would be our little secret. When he walked into the visiting room the attraction we had for each other was undeniable. We hugged, kissed and talked for hours after the visit. I told him if no one comes to see him that I will be the one and here we are today.

FP) How much time did he have remaining on his sentence?

AJ) In the beginning he told me two years and then he told me the truth. He had five years left on his sentence.

"I was all in, I wanted to see how this would turn out." - Andrea Jackson

FP) You were willing to do 5 years with him, you're the true definition of a ride or die.

AJ) I was all in, I wanted to see how this would turn out. I wanted to put my all into it and give it a chance. To get back to your original question, he started the business One Source FInancial Inc. That's one of the things I love about him. He will always come up with ideas to make money. I always wanted to start my own business. I was married for 10 years and always wanted a sports bar, but never got any support from my ex-husband. So when I saw we were both business-minded the attraction grew stronger. He was fixing inmates' credit and their loved ones at the time. Then he wanted to expand to the people on the outside and to other institutions and he needed help with that. We had to get a website built. At the time I was making 6-figures as a property manager, so I was able to help him move forward with his endeavors. So along with the credit repair he wanted to add taxes. I don't know anything about taxes or credit repair, but I believed in him.

So we had to get an EFIN number for the business through the IRS. We submitted the application, but due to the government shut down in 2018-2019 the process was long.

FP) What is an EFIN number?

AJ) One EFIN is needed for every firm or physical location from which you file tax returns for clients. If you're filing more than 10 tax returns each year, you'll need an EFIN whether you're working as a sole practitioner or own the business. So we had to partner with another company and use their EFIN number, so that was cutting into our profits. You have to remember, I had a full time job, on top of that I was interviewing people for the job as a tax preparer, finding partners for the credit repair and really putting this company together.

FP) So how did you market your company?

AJ) We would put it on different social media sites. Me being a property manager, I would go to different properties and ask to set up to do their tenants' taxes. Other tax preps used to come to my property and do taxes for my tenants.

AJ) I used to do this in Maryland and New Jersey so I had support in those states. We started building our team. After tax season, we needed another stream of income. So he wanted to sell insurance too. He has an uncle who is a life insurance agent so we partnered with him. It didn't work out with his uncle though. His goals weren't aligned with One Source Financial Inc so we parted ways.

I must say, I learned a lot from him. I learned about marketing leads and who to go through to get licensing. When the pandemic hit it was the perfect opportunity for me to get my insurance license. At the time, I still had my 9 to 5, so I would work my job and run the company simultaneously, and then go home and study. The test was hard, I failed the first time. The second test was for life insurance and health, I passed them both. I really didn't like life and health, it was too depressing to talk about death. One day a gentleman called and asked if I had my property & casualty license. I didn't know what that was at the time. He explained that I would be able to sell auto, home, renters, commercial trucking, and business. I thought that would be much better for me, I couldn't wait for my baby to call so I could run it by him. When I spoke with him he told me to get all my licenses, so I had to do more studying. So now I have all my licenses but don't know what to do with them. I have no experience at all, I was so confused.

So I left my job to work for Allstate making $1000 and 3% commission every two weeks. I was on my own for about a month before my baby got immediate release and came home.

FP) Why couldn't you work the insurance job part-time?

AJ)That's how I started it, the business was the side hustle and I had my primary job. It was a tough decision because I had a stable income every two weeks and selling insurance is commission-based. I needed to focus more on my business if I wanted it to succeed. So I saved up some money and left property management. Spending habits changed for the both of us, we were on a tight budget.

FP) So how hard was it for you to do the time with your fiance?

AJ) Going to visit him was hard. The first time I went to visit I thought I was early, but I was actually late because they started count. Count time is when CO's count the inmates. During the weekend count starts around 10 am. If you don't get there before count starts, you will be waiting a long time to get in for your visit. I told myself, 'I need to figure out how all this works." Since I was going to be doing the time with him. I found out from the other women how to get in early. I used to leave my house at like 2 am to get there early so I could be one of the first one's there. I was driving from Maryland to South Jersey. That was about a three hour drive.

I used to sleep in my car waiting to get in. There were two lines: the first line was for cars and then there was a line to stand in, waiting to get inside the building. Try standing in that line during the winter time. Everyone is frustrated. The CO's talk to you like you're the criminal, women trying to cut the line, after you sacrifice your sleep and time to get there early. One time I Got into it with a woman. It wasn't anything physical because the CO's and the captain got in the middle of it. She had a friend in line already and tried to cut the line to jump in with her friend. Some women let it happen but I had to speak up. You have to speak up, so they know that you're not taking no shit.

AJ) I used to visit so much I didn't have to show my ID anymore. When you go visit someone consistently at the same time and day, it's usually the same people who see you every weekend. You start to build relationships with the other women because you have something in common. We became each other's support. There were times when I would miss his calls or when he'd ask me to do things for him and it might not get done at the time he wanted it. So he would call with an attitude and frustrate me more.

I had to let him know I had other things out here that I was doing. I also have a life out here. I have my children I have to attend to, my work, the business and him. It's only only 24 hours in a day and I also have to sleep. So if I missed a call or didn't get something done right away, I needed him to understand not to get upset. He was getting there. It was a growth process for him because he was so spoiled. I was overwhelming, but then he started to get better with it. Now that he's home, he sees how much work it is and appreciates me more.

Now let's talk about money. He's very prideful. In the beginning, he wouldn't take anything from me. Who doesn't need extra money!? So I would just put money on his books. He had some hustle in there because he always had money coming to my cash app but I didn't like it, so I told him whatever he's doing, to stop and I'll take care of him. His spending limit was $360.00 a month, I made sure he had that and on top of what his friends and family were sending him. He was more than good. It was really really tough, but I was very determined. That's what type of person I am. I had down periods, because like I said it was just overwhelming at times, and he knew that. He would rejuvenate me and I would be right back at it. He used to keep me going, he definitely motivated me.

FP) How did your family and friends feel about your new man?

AJ) They knew a little bit about him, but didn't know he was from Jersey and didn't know he was in prison. I was hiding him. I love him so much. I wanted everyone to know about him. I have a Facebook page with all my friends and family on there and they boogie as hell and are very judgemental. Every time I used to hang out with them and he called, I would step outside so they would be like 'Who is this man? Why haven't we ever met him?' I would be like 'You will meet him. He lives in NJ.' I would be lying and telling more lies on top of lies. It became hard to keep up with the lies, so I stopped hanging out with them because I was afraid my lies would catch up with me. It was too much pressure. One day I posted a picture of him on my

Facebook page and of course he was in prison. At first I would just post a headshot to hide the fact that he was in prison. After a while I would get bold and show his full body. My phone started to ring off the hook. My inbox started to blow up so I pulled down my Facebook page and that caused me to lose family and friends. They would say things like 'Who is this guy? Why is he locked up? You can do better than that. You're better than that. He's just using you. It's jail talk.'

I would get mad and curse their asses out. The negative thoughts would pop up in my head and I would ask myself, 'Are they right!? Is he using me!?' When you hear it from everyone you start to believe it. The only person who had anything nice to say about it was my mother. She told me to take all the negative things that people say about you and use it as fuel. Even if it doesn't work out, at least you gain more business knowledge and become an owner of a business.

She also said she doesn't think someone would partner with anyone who he's going to leave because my name is on everything. She told me to keep doing what I'm doing and that's what I did. It was really tough, knowing all the backlash I was going to get and I got it because I probably would've been the same way if one of my friends told me they met someone in prison.

The man I met is cool as shit and because of him I don't judge anyone in prison. He opened up my eyes to a lot and we're still cool to this day. It's hard for us on the outside. What they need to understand is that we're doing the time also and it's hard. The drive, the gas, you have to pay a toll, even if you have to fly, everything costs money.

If your money is funny it's even harder. Sometimes I came to visit with $10, sometimes $30 and we had to make it work. To all the men and women who are incarcerated, 'When you call and don't get an answer or if you ask someone to do something and it doesn't get done right away, don't start an argument, show some appreciation, don't make them feel like they're not appreciated. We go through standing out in the snow, rain, cold, waiting to get inside; the CO's see all of this and they don't care. They try to hit on us, break us, discourage us from coming back. Old ladies with canes, babies...they're not letting anyone in until it's time to come through that door. So yeah, it's hard doing time, so work with us, stop acting like we are the ones who put you in there.

FP) You also started a cleaning company while he was incarcerated?

Yes, he was overwhelming. He knew I was a property manager and I hired cleaning companies to clean the property. So instead of hiring a cleaning company I could just hire ours. Business was picking up and it was going pretty well until COVID hit, so then we had to put it on pause. The good thing about COVID is he got out two years early. We knew he had a decent judge because he lost trial and only got 151 months, so we gave it a shot. He sent a motion in and the judge gave him a public defender. Then six months later he got immediate release. Remember I quit my job, so by then I was working for AllState, making $1000 every two weeks. Our budget was really tight now. Now he's home to help me so I don't have to wear all the hats. When he first came home we started back up the cleaning service, but it was too much work trying to run two businesses simultaneously, so we sold the cleaning service. I stayed with Allstate for a few more weeks, learned everything that I could and here we are today.

FP) So you are not working for Allstate anymore? Why didn't you just open up own Allstate agency?

AJ) It cost $100,000 to open up an Allstate agency and you can only sell their products. Our agency is independent so we're able to sell different agency products, which leads us to finding the best rates customize to your needs.

> "We go through standing out in the snow, rain, cold, waiting to get inside; the CO's see all of this and they don't care."

FP) How do you get to sell products for other agencies?

AJ) When I was working for Allstate, he thought I was there for the long haul, but my fiance sent me there as a spy. That's what he told me to keep me motivated because the pay was crap. I had to remember the reason I was there and that was to pick their brain and get all the information I would need for our business. I had to get appointed by the carriers and most insurance carriers want you to build a book of business. A book of business is basically all the insurance products you sold, how much money you have with the business. At the time I had 0. I didn't think these carriers would do business with me, with my business just starting out. I would send out emails to Progressive, Liberty Mutual, Encompass, Metlife, and a whole lot more trying to get them to partner with my company. I had to convince them that I was going to bring them business. Due to the pandemic, they would interview me through Zoom and I would convince them that I would bring them no less than $25,000 a year in premiums and become an agent for that particular company. I was determined to make this work because I knew how much money I made solely depended on me. When I worked for Allstate I would bring in a nice piece of premium and look at my check and it did not add up.

FP) So is One Source Financial Inc. an insurance agency?

AJ) No, the insurance agency is called Source One Insurance Agency. It's a subsidy of One Source Financial Inc, and now that my fiance is home, it's nothing stopping us.

Letter from an Inmate

WRITTEN BY TORRY T. DAVIS

Greetings,

My name is Torry T. Davis and I am currently being held at FCI Edgefield in South Carolina. Back in 2014, I was sentenced and I am just a couple of years from being released. Prior to my incarceration, I was attending a technical college for the attainment of my associates degree in Business Management. Back then, my plan was to open my own apparel store and grow it into retail chains in the Southeast region. However, I still had one foot in the drug trade and was indicted by the feds. During my incarceration, I have had the opportunity to focus on my individuality so I can start the journey to reinventing myself to become the person I always knew I wanted to be. Since being here, I have gained experience in manufacturing garments such as tee shirts, military trousers, sweatsuits, and handbags for government agencies. I also completed classes to earn credentials for skills such as Lean Six Sigma. Due to my work ethic, I was promoted from sewing operator to the Quality Assurance department as a quality inspector and I learned so much about the importance of sustainable garments and Grade A stitching. With my passion in upscale street culture, sports, art, and music coupled with my aspirations for styling and engaging in a better quality of life, I decided to build my own fashion brand. I have 80% of my business plan written (due to limited information) and I have the vision for how to network and accumulate more capital to start my venture.

Until I can get the resources I need I will continue to study business structure, branding, and fashion until I'm released. I wrote to say I appreciate the emails and opportunity you guys are giving to people like me who aspire to make changes in our respective communities. Not only do I need mentorship from this company now I would love to come out and work with you all on building my empire. I'm all in with whatever tools you have to offer because no matter the circumstances I still have my intuition even when my vision feels impaired so the future starts now.

follow your passion.

Entrepreneur Highlight

FEATURING RULER

I have been tattooing about 26 years, I hope I didn't give up my age. It kind of just happened. A lot of my friends used to come to me like, 'Yo, Bra, I want to get this tattoo. Can you draw something for me? I either drew it for them or literally drew it on them. I had no intentions of becoming a tattoo artist. It didn't even cross my mind. The owner of the shop, was like 'Who the fuck is drawing these pictures? We set up a meeting and he gave me a free apprenticeship. I was in the program for a year and I couldn't touch anyone's skin. I would clean up, run errands to the store and just watch. Just hangout in the shop with no pay. You learn a lot being around the game. I was drawing for the tattoo artist so I was able to make some money during that time.

Then a year later I got my shot. I came in right on time. Back then you will just walk into a shop and look at the flash. There were posted images of tattoo designs that you can find on the walls of almost every tattoo shop in the world known as "flash," which is a name that comes from a time during the start of tattooing, when artists had to work on the move. Tattooing wasn't mainstream. Now everybody and their mother has a tattoo or is doing tattoos.

When I got into the game there were only a few shops doing custom designs and we were one of them. Custom tattoos can be something you describe or a picture you like and it allows me to take creative rights over. A custom design is best if you want a tattoo that is unique to you or holds a lot of meaning. With the flash tattoo you can walk out of the shop with everyone having the same tattoo as you. Money was really good when custom tattooing hit the market.

"Tattooing wasn't mainstream. Now everybody is doing it."

It was something new, something different. People were getting flash tattoos. They were small and it wasn't meaningful, it didn't hold sentimental value to the individual. When a customer thinks of something they want and asks you to draw it up and then put it on their body, it changes the game. It's Business 101: supply and demand.

A lot of tattoo shops weren't doing it then, so we were eating real good. While a lot of my guys were selling dope I was selling Ink. I look back at the time and always kick myself in the ass for not saving. My money wasn't on the books, at the time I was buying everything, spending money like crazy.

My current price for a tattoo is $200 a hour. Being that tattoos are more accepted now you wouldn't think it's more money now than every before. Not for me currently but the industry as a whole, yes. Let me give you an example. When marijuana was called ses street guys were making a lot more money than you can make now, but as an industry, marijuana is more lucrative than ever. Everyone is selling that "Za Za." I'm still eating but nothing like when custom design hit the market.

INTERESTED IN INK?

You have to put a portfolio together. Another name for it is a work sketch. It's really hard to get into an apprenticeship program. You have to be good. You could open your own shop if you wanted to bypass working for someone else, but I would recommend working in a shop first. Get all the experience you can before you open your shop, just keep that to yourself because owners hate that you learn what you can then leave.

Final Words

Whatever you're trying to do, just stay focus even when times get hard and you will prevail.

21 BEST SIDE HUSTLES

TO EARN EXTRA INCOME

Side hustles are a productive way to make some extra money, especially if you're looking to make extra money to complement your main job. We here at Financial Playaz, believe in the accumulated power of racking up numerous side hustles; diversifying your source of income can protect your wealth by helping you pay off bills or debt, save up for the house you always wanted. When signing up for side hustles, it's important to know what they are – just side hustles and nothing more. These short and easy gigs probably won't help you earn as much as your primary job, and it may take you longer to earn something remotely substantial.

01 Niche blog

If you have access to a computer and expertise, blogging is an excellent way to make passive income. If you have no experience with SEO, you may have a hard time attracting traffic. Carve out time to learn SEO tactics so you can better direct readers to your website.

02 Real Estate

Set goals and invest and diversify your money into projects, with each tailored to help you grow your net worth. A tip: you need to do your own due diligence when investing, so if you're not familiar with real estate investing, you must proceed with caution.

03 Earn $ Online

Earn money online for completing an array of online activities that include watching videos, answering surveys, playing games, or reading promotional emails. There are varies ways to earn money online. It may be hard to qualify for surveys.

04 Deliver takeout

There are several driver delivery apps, you can choose your own hours and work where you want as long as you have your method for delivery. You get to keep 100% of your tips so there's an upside to your earnings potential. You can make decent money along the way.

05 Paid Surveys

Websites capitalize on a company's need for market research by building a community of survey-takers. If you have time to spare, it is a great way to make extra change. Surveys come with pre qualifying questions to determine your eligibility.

06 Search engine

Changing your default search engine is an easy way to make a little passive income. After signing up, you can download the web browser, surf the web like you normally do, and start making money. New users instantly receive a $10 sign up bonus.

07 Niche blog

Earn cashback for around 2,500 stores including Walmart, Target, Amazon, and Kohl's. After logging in, simply find the store you want to shop in on the website, select 'Double Cash-Back Stores', and get your shopping on. It's absolutely free. You'll get paid every three months.

08 Delivery courier

Couriers are tasked with delivering groceries, food, or even booze. You can use a bike for deliveries if you don't have a car. There aren't any startup fees or time commitments so you can work on your own time. A great choice for young people who want to make more than the minimum wage.

09 Grow audience

Grow your online business and earn more from it. You can create email campaigns and sign up forms, manage your subscribers, view analytics reports, and create an image library. If you have a blog, online store, or a business, email marketing can be a powerful tool to help you earn more!

10 Freelance

If you have expertise in graphics and design, business, digital marketing, lifestyle, writing, video and animation, music and audio, or programming and tech, then someone is looking for you. There are many online marketplaces for freelancer services.

11 Deliver groceries

The goal is to fulfill these requests by picking out goods and delivering them to the customer's door. Shoppers are compensated via a formula that considers the number of orders per shift along with the number of items per order + tips. You can set your hours or log in anytime.

12 Share data

Share your data with a global measurement and data analytics company. Be rewarded for allowing data and software companies to anonymously collect your browsing history from your web-surfing device. The software won't hamper the speed of your computer.

13 Dog sit

Pet lovers can diversify their services for even more earnings. You can host dogs in your home while walking others on your lunch break and stopping over houses on your way home to feed pets a few times a week. You may also need typical pet supplies such as toys, a crate, extra leashes, and poop bags.

14 Lose weight

When it comes to weight loss, money can be a powerful motivation. You can bet on your weight loss and compete against others, either as a team or individually. If you reach your weight loss goal, you'll get paid in cash. This is an easy way to earn money if you're determined to lose weight.

15 Rent out car

If your car's collecting cobwebs in your garage, why not just rent it out and make some extra money? If you agree to the customer's request, you'll meet with the renter, check their license, make a note of your mileage and fuel, and hand over the keys

16 $ for opinions

Share your opinions with market research companies to earn cash instead of points! You can earn moneyfor participating in surveys, watching videos, and reading promotional emails. You can only cash out once you've reached $50.

17 Trade stocks

Thinking about stocks for your side hustle? Invest in trade options, stocks, cryptocurrency, and exchange-traded funds without the need to pay fees or commissions. You can even earn free stock simply by signing up and inviting others.

18 Online games

Earn points for playing games, watching videos, and visiting other websites. Rack up points to earn cash, which you can use for travel miles, gift cards, or PayPal cash. Only available for residents of Canada and the US.

19 Deliver food

Deliver food in your spare time and unlike a pizza-delivery job, you have the entire hood as your clientele.you can set your own hours and cash out your earnings on the same day – this gives you the flexibility of working only when you want, making it a great side hustle for those who already have primary jobs.

20 Online sales

If you're looking to sell your skills online, you need a strong online presence. Once you've created a website that perfectly represents your brand, a number of tools to help you capture leads are in your disposal: create a sign-up page for an event, a freebie, pop-up boxes, sales pages for products and services and much more!

21 Rent out space

If you have an extra space you can make passive income out of it. The process is simple: check out how much your space is worth, list your room or entire house, screen potential guests, and then get paid. You can post images, set your price, and availability dates. You can also draft house rules to make sure everyone respects your space.

Financial Playaz

If you have something positive going on and you want to share it with the Financial Playaz or if there is something that you want to learn or know about you can write to us at P.O. Box 8781 Elkridge, MD 21075.

One Source Financial Inc.

If you need your credit fix or in need for tradelines, you can write to us at P.O. Box 8781 Elkridge, MD 21075, email us at onesourcefinancialinc@gmail.com or contact us at (800) 654-9901.

I have helped many other inmates and have had success in assisting them in fixing their credit correctly! I can help you too!

Economics of Drug Selling

This report was written by Ryan King, Policy Analyst for The Sentencing Project, with editorial assistance from Marc Mauer.

Overall, three sophisticated studies have addressed the economics of the drug trade. Levitt and Venkatesh (2000) used a unique set of data to provide significant insight into the drug selling economy. 1 They combined interview responses with financial data (costs, revenue, price, quantity) that were kept by a gang leader in order to manage a distribution network.

This offered the researchers the opportunity to track, over time, how money flowed, and to whom, within a drug market. A second study, sponsored by RAND, looked at persons engaged in the sale of drugs in Washington, DC.2 The authors combined interviews of drug sellers with arrest data, offense history, personal demographics, education, and employment. A third study, in Wisconsin, examined drug markets by placing them in the larger context of the conventional labor market, paying particular attention to the fluid movement between illicit and legal forms of employment.

Ryan King is a Senior Fellow at the Urban Institute and has many published articles and previously worked for the Sentencing Project. Learn more about him urban.org.

OVERVIEW

The economics of the illicit drug market in the United States have been a source of much speculation and misinformation. A key reason for this lack of knowledge relates to the inherent nature of drug selling. Drug distribution is an illegal business venture, and is therefore cloaked in secrecy in order to protect the participants who are engaged in what is often a dangerous enterprise. Because of the concealed nature of drug markets, few researchers have been able to penetrate their boundaries and gain the trust of participants in order to observe and describe these networks.

This briefing paper surveys the relative handful of studies that have been able to evaluate the workings of drug markets. These include data analyses of drug gang finances, surveys of convicted drug offenders, and ethnographic studies involving interviews with drug sellers. The findings of these various studies generally indicate that drug selling, while clearly illegal, shares many characteristics of other business enterprises. Further, many of the commonly held perceptions regarding the lucrative nature of the drug trade turn out to be significantly exaggerated.

EARNINGS

Overall, all three studies conclude that the average earnings of a person working in the drug trade are far less than have been traditionally perceived. At the top of the drug hierarchy, earnings can be very substantial. The Levitt and Venkatesh study estimates that annual earnings for drug gang leaders are between $50,000 and $130,000.4 This is clearly significantly higher than these individuals could earn locally in the legitimate labor market. However, very few people in any given drug market make these wages. The Officers, the second level of the hierarchy, are estimated to earn $12,000 per year, or slightly higher than minimum wage for a full-time job. The lowest level of the hierarchy, and the most prevalent, are the street level sellers. These are the individuals who are actively engaged in the daily sale of drugs, and who are generally paid based upon the amount of product they dispense. On average, street dealers make less than $2500 per year. Even though they only work approximately 20 hours per week, their pay level is still far below the minimum wage. The fact that the job requires minimal skills,with a veritable army of reserves waiting to fill in any job opening, puts consistent downward pressure on wages for street level dealers. The authors of this study conclude, despite the radical skewing of the wage distribution, that on average, the earnings of individuals involved in drug dealing are not appreciably higher than available market alternatives. But this average figure is raised significantly by the relative handful of high level dealers who are making substantial wages. Therefore, a question that arises is: if wages are so low for low-level drug dealers, why would they be willing to engage in such high-risk labor rather than working in the safer and higher paying legitimate economy? Researchers Levitt and Venkatesh conclude that the desire to move up through the hierarchy and make the earnings of gang leaders is sufficient motivation for sellers to "pay their dues" by laboring in the low end of the wage spectrum. The two other studies under review have come to similar conclusions. In the analysis of Washington, DC markets, RAND researchers concluded that the median earnings for those engaged in drug selling were $721 per month. 5 These figures varied significantly based on how much time the individual spent in this pursuit. The average respondent reported a net income of $700 per month from drug sales, with a range from $25 for the small earner to $2500 for the typical large earner.6 For the people who sold daily, a fraction of the sample, the median net earnings were $2000 per month. Based upon their limited working hours, this translates into an hourly wage of $30. Research in Wisconsin by John Hagedorn also reported earnings that varied based upon the amount of time spent on drug dealing. Of the sample interviewed, a third made less than or equal to minimum wage, one-third made in the range of $13 to $25 per hour and a handful reported making in excess of $10,000 per month. 7 Hagedorn concludes that the majority of drug dealers in his case study in Milwaukee earned (gross) between $1000 and $5000 per month, and worked long hours in order to achieve this wage. Oftentimes, this income was supplemented by wages from the legitimate sector.

TIME SPENT SELLING DRUGS

Two of the three studies examined conclude that drug dealing is far less of an all encompassing economic pursuit than many have speculated. Very few dealers spend all of their working time selling drugs and most have some form of legitimate employment for which they use drug dealing as a means of supplementing income. In the Washington, DC study group, most individuals were selling drugs on a part-time basis. Close to 25% of the sample sold drugs no more than once a week, and these people reported monthly net earnings from the drug trade of just $50 a month. About three-eighths sold daily, with a median gross income of $3600 per month, and a median net income of about $2000. Typically, people in this sample spent about three hours a day selling drugs, averaging about 13 sales per day. In Wisconsin, about 50% of those who had reported having sold cocaine sold in no more than 12 months out of the previous 36 months. Only slightly over 1 in 10 sold more than 24 out of the past 36 months.

OTHER EMPLOYMENT

All three studies conclude that the persons involved in drug sales were sporadically moving in and out of legal and illegal employment markets. In Milwaukee, Hagedorn observed that few individuals earned their income solely from sales of illegal drugs; rather, they used the income to supplement legal employment, which often paid a wage that was unable to meet their needs. In Washington, DC, three-quarters of the sample had some form of legitimate work during the period studied. The median monthly income from that job was approximately $800. In analyzing arrest data in Washington DC, the authors found that of those charged with possession, 74% were employed and of those charged with a drug sale, 67% were otherwise employed.

They concluded that drug selling was not a specialized industry, and was a complement to, rather than a substitute for, legitimate employment. Levitt and Venkatesh report similar figures, estimating that 75-80% held low-paying jobs in the legitimate sector at some point throughout the year.

CHARACTERISTICS OF DRUG MARKETS

The handful of studies on the economics of illicit narcotics markets indicate several common characteristics: 1-Few drug sellers are making substantial earnings. Most use drug dealing as a supplement to wages made in the legitimate sector, raising questions about the availability of economic opportunity in low-income urban communities. 2-Most drug dealers spend a fraction of their time selling drugs, but are forced to work significant hours in order to attain these earnings. 3-The drug market is a perpetually fluid situation, and most individuals' careers are very short, with earnings often fleeting. Hagedorn reported that most drug dealers were on what he characterized as an economic merry-go-round in which they rotated in and out of the legitimate and illegitimate earnings sector. Levitt and Venkatesh also noted that most of the drug dealers they had interviewed for their study had since abandoned the trade. 4-Most of those in the drug trade are not generally engaged in violence. Authors of the Washington, DC study concluded that only about one-quarter of their sample had ever been arrested for a violent crime, and about one-sixth had been convicted of a violent crime. Hagedorn posits that violent activity is most likely to occur as new markets emerge, but as they reach a point of stasis, violence decreases. The longer markets remain in operation, the less likelihood that violence will occur.

Those surveyed in Milwaukee reported no daily occurrences of violence, and most reported only occasional incidence of violence. This should come as little surprise, as violence and disruption are intimately linked, and business (licit or illicit) does not like disruption. 5- The profile of drug offenders in prison confirms that, to a large extent, lower-level drug users and sellers represent a substantial portion of persons convicted and sentenced to prison. Analysis of the most recent data available (1997) indicates that of those currently incarcerated on a drug charge, 58% have no history of violence or high-level drug activity and three-quarters have a criminal record of only drug charges or other non-violent offenses.9 6-Those who patronize drug markets, according to evidence from Milwaukee, are primarily from outside the neighborhood where drugs are being sold. Only a small minority of persons buying drugs resided in the proximate neighborhood, and a significant percentage of consumers in this urban market were white. Hagedorn also concludes, in his comparison of urban (minority) and suburban drug markets (white), that the suburban drug market is far larger, despite the fact that this is not represented in arrest data. 7-The values and ideals espoused by the respondents in these studies closely mirror those that are reported to be held by most Americans. Hagedorn concludes that conventional values can coexist within the drug market, as selling is simply seen as work, and not crime. He contends that 9 King, R.S. & Mauer, M. (2002). "Distorted Priorities: that 9 King, R.S. & Mauer, M. (2002). "Distorted Priorities: Drug Offenders in State Prisons." Washington, DC: The Sentencing Project. 5 persons working in the drug market are seeking to attain the core values of "the American way of life." Levitt and Venkatesh agree, concluding that the reason that many are willing to work in such a dangerous enterprise for such low pay

is the belief that they are "paying their dues" and they will "move up the ladder" and fulfill "the American dream." The common thread that runs through these reports is that drug dealing is a transitory enterprise, undertaken periodically by individuals struggling to survive and viewing it as a means of supplementing income in order to help propel them towards attaining their personal goals. This raises the question of the role of incarceration in dealing with drug markets. An alternative approach would be to address the issue of economic development in urban neighborhoods. In this regard, drug dealing can be seen not as a cause of urban decline, but rather as a response to the evaporation of a sustainable employment market with the exodus of manufacturing and commerce from urban areas beginning in the 1960s.

TIME IS MONEY. INVEST IT IN YOUR EDUCATION AND EARN UNLIMITED INTEREST!!

"I'm not a Businessman.. I'm a Business Man!" -JAY-Z

This powerful affirmation by Jay-Z was intended to impress on the minds of listeners the distinction between those who are employed in the business of trade - and those who are the Business in trade! The distinction is, like all things, rooted in your thought & behavior patterns. While financial literacy indicates one has learned [about] finance.. it does not mean one [IS] actively living, breathing, eating, and sleeping Finance! If you want to experience a drastic shift in your financial condition, you must actively and consciously choose to learn what the wealthy know that you don't... [AND] actively and consciously choose to [EMBODY] what you have learned.

In other words, you must walk it like you talk it, day in & day out, without a doubt. Of course, this process begins when you consciously manage your Greatest asset of all...YOUR TIME. Investing your time in educating yourself on the habits of the wealthy and then actively putting that knowledge to daily use is the MISSION of the 100MILLMVMT.

The 100MILLMVMT is a collective mission of only highly motivated individuals who are dedicated to the education, guidance, motivation and birth of 100 millionaires!! The members of the 100MILLMVMT will be actively participating in a series of workshops which will be delivered online. Each Workshop will progressively guide each member through every step they need to build their business credit and reach a minimum buying/investing power of $1,000,000.00. The workshops are specifically designed for you to learn the steps and then actively employ the steps. So, it is ACTION based at its core. If you are serious about drastically changing your financial future for you and your family, and you are about that ACTION and want to learn how to get started then sign up by sending an email to: onesourcefinancialinc@gmail.com

King Truck: Make $250,000 A Year With A Criminal Record & No College Degree

Words and photos by Shawn Williams

I titled my book, *Make $250,000 A Year With A Criminal Record And No College Degree!!!* A lot of people say they can't find a job because of their record, so we eliminate that. In order to get a good job you have to go to college and get a degree, we eliminated that. So I show them how to make $5,000 to $7,000 a week and in recent times because of COVID it's better now. You make anywhere between $8,000 to $12,000 a week. I made $11,000 this week, that's half a million a year. $10,000 times 52 weeks, you do the math.

I would get the newspaper and scan the classified ads. I saw that there were one or two jobs for HVAC, plumbing, electrical and then 70 trucking jobs paying $60,000 with a $5,000 sign on bonus so I said that's where the opportunity is. While I was still in prison, I met someone who owned their own truck. You can be anybody you want to be in prison, especially if you are from out of town. He was from North Carolina and I listened to him. I took notes and what he was talking about and he had a magazine that sold trucks

so that really got me amped up. When I came home I went straight to school. I went to All State. It was a 6-month program. It cost me $10,000 back then, it's about $12,000 right now, but that's how I got started. It was a grind. While I was in school for 6 months, I was working for Burger King, telemarketing my first job making $18 dollars a day. I was flagging for a temp agency (That's the stop and go sign). I was doing that on the weekend making $70.00 a day and I was selling chips, soda and candy while I was in school.

When I graduated they had a career services office, so they hooked me up with a construction job and they had small dump trucks and smaller trailers that haul equipment. I was doing that for nine months. From working at Burger King I went to deliver pizza for Domino's. I eventually replaced Domino's and I started driving limos, which I did for seven years. I bought a bus and converted it into a mega party bus. Instead of the bus fitting 15 to 16 people, it now fits 32 people with seven stripper poles for a private sector. It has been a constant progression, also with a lot of setbacks along the way.

I learned a lot from Master P. I took a Masterclass with him in New York and I got a chance to ask him which way to go, 'Do I go nationwide or stay local?' He said, "Take 10% of everything you make and dominate your area first, because before you start branching off you will have a solid foundation." So I've been implementing that. I spend way more than 10%. I spend about $900 a week in marketing. I do it because when you're in the streets you become hood washed to what you say everyday, through music, movies you're influenced by your friends. You have to reprogram your mind so I became a self help junkie. I started reading every book I could get my hands on, I paid to go to all the seminars and I noticed that a lot of that stuff is gimmicky, because if they were really trying to help people why are they charging $3,000 to sit in a class for a weekend, just to tell me the stuff you said in your book. Now the books I have, you can purchase, but I don't sell them. What I mean by that is, I have them for purchase but I give most of them away.

Everything doesn't boil down to a dollar amount. If you have it in your heart to really help people that's what you're for, but a lot of people are caught in what I call the chitlin circuit. They sit there and sell hope to people and then they string them along. At first you will go to the free event, when you get to the free event then they are going to sell you the mentor, which is three to five thousand a year, one phone call a month. Then they're going to try to sell you the boat cruise which is $40,000 and it's constant over and over again. My lawyer recommended a book called Think And Grow Rich by Napoleon Hill.

So throughout the journey, I realized that everyone was using his philosophy so I purchased all his bo-

-oks and even joined the Napoleon Hill Foundation and got trained by them. I'm actually a master teacher in that philosophy, and it works. It doesn't work overnight, but it works.

It takes time, you have to endure the downfalls. I lost a lot of money. I went through 17 to 18 trucks, I had trucks that were in floods, trucks that blew up. I have been an owner operator and getting trucks too fast and dispatches be slowing you up on loads. I had my authority and didn't know what to do with it, nobody to call. I had to sit for six years while trying to figure it out. What took 10 years for me, it can be done in less than two years and it's all in this book, *Make $250,000 A Year With A Criminal Record And No College Degree*.

All you have to do is follow step by step. It's three levels within trucking: company driver, owner operator, and own authority. Company driver drives for the company and has no investment, that's a job. The owner operator owns the truck but they don't own the company, the company gives them a load and gives them a split 70/30 or 75/25. The third is when you get your own authority: when you have your own truck, trailer and insure your company and book your own loads and keep 100% of the load. So the difference is that a company driver makes about $900 to $1200 a week, $1500 to 1600 when it's bumping in the summertime. Owner operator makes about $2,500 to $3,500. Own authority during normal circumstances $5000 to $7,000 a week. Right now we're making $8,000 to $12,000. I'm not going to lie to you, the past month I made $50,000 by myself in a rented day cab with no bed in it driving across the country.

All the money is in doing the driving. People get this misconception that the money is in getting trucks, hiring a driver and going to sleep. It doesn't work like that.

Another thing people try to duplicate themselves when you get another truck, but you're not because nobody is going to work hard like you. When you hire someone you essentially take on their problems. If they got child support, crazy girlfriends, if they have a wife that is worrying about cheating on them, if they have a warrant, a drug problem. All of them are problems you're taking on. *Continued on page 31*

TOP TEN PAYING JOBS FOR FELONS

Welding

Many convicted felons find that welding is a rewarding career. As a welder, you can perform a range of welding tasks depending on where you live and the area in which you would like to specialize. Most welders earn around $41,380 per year, but you could make as little as $25,000 per year if you don't have much experience. If you choose to increase your skills and specialize in an in-demand field, you could earn up to $60,000 per year or more. Welding careers offer many chances to advance yourself as long as you make an effort to improve and grow.

Electrician

If you need a job as a felon, consider working as an electrician. Qualified electricians earn an average of $55,000 per year, and experts believe the demand for electricians will rise by 14 percent over the next 10 years. You work indoors and outside when you choose this career option. You install, maintain and repair electrical systems for homes, businesses and government buildings depending on the company for which you work. Check the local laws in your area before moving forward if you don't want to run into any unexpected problems along the way.

HVAC Technician

As a felon, working as an HVAC technician is a viable option worth considering. If you select this option, you can expect an average pay of $47,610 each year. Occupational professionals expect this career to grow by 15 percent between 2016 and 2026. HVAC experts install, replace and repair heating, ventilating and air conditioning systems in a variety of settings. You could work in homes, offices, schools, factories, hospitals and more. You can go to a trade school to get an early start on this path, or you can opt for on-the-job training. You will dedicate a lot of time and effort to this career if you choose it.

Carpenter

Those seeking jobs for felons that pay well often choose carpentry to reach their goals. This career offers a median pay of $46,509 per year and has an average growth outlook.

Choose this path if you want a career that offers stable employment and the opportunity to advance. Some people jump into this career path before they fully understand what it requires of them. You can also try going to a trade school in your area if you would like to boost your skills to the next level. Like many of the other jobs listed in this guide, you can use the skills you learn to launch a carpentry business of your own one day.

Military

Although some people think they can't join the military with a felony conviction, that is not always the case. The military looks at a variety of factors when deciding whether or not it will let you join their ranks. If you are searching for salary and job growth information, you will be disappointed to learn that no one answer gives the full picture. If you want to pursue a military career with a felony conviction on your background report, speaking with your recruiter is the first step in your journey. For obvious reasons, the military prefers recruiting people of high moral standards.

Oil Field Jobs

Even though many companies are turning to wind and solar power, fossil fuels will remain relevant for years to come. Since the demand for oil and gas shows no sign of slowing down, oil field jobs are a great choice for felons who are willing to work hard each day. The pay and job outlook depend on the exact position you try obtaining. Oil rig operators can expect to make around $50,000 per year, and many support positions earn similar wages. If you set your sights high and become a petroleum engineer, wages of $65 per hour could be in your future.

Truck Driver

The influx of people buying items online over the past few years has increased the demand for truck drivers across the nation. Commercial truck driving is often stressful, and this stress contributes to the high turnover rate. The turnover rate, however, is good for you because it means trucking companies are always desperate for new drivers. If you have a commercial driver's license and show a willingness to work hard, you won't have trouble getting a job. This career is not for you if you don't enjoy being away from home for extended periods. The average wage is $43,690 per year. While many truck drivers opt to work overtime to increase their income, they can work no more than 14 hours per day. Many truck drivers stay away from their hometowns for days or weeks before returning. That is why truck driving is not just a career; it's a lifestyle choice.

Marketing

Marketing is another one of the top high-paying jobs for felons, and it could be the right option for you. Marketers earn an average wage of $132,000 per year. When you work as a marketer, you help companies create sales material that connects with their target audience on a deep level and compels them to buy. You do market research to learn the demand for the products or services your employer sells, and you then learn about the most pressing needs and desires of their ideal customer. Using that information, you improve your company's profit by creating advertisements that get results and grab attention.

Entrepreneur

Many criminals are creative and determined individuals who need a healthy way to channel their energy. If you take those abilities and point them in the right direction, you will often get entrepreneurs. The best part of being an entrepreneur is that you decide what requirements you have to meet to move forward. When you work for someone else, the human resources department looks at your application and background to decide if it should hire you. As an entrepreneur, the people who hire you look at your skill and the results you can achieve for them. his option could be a smart choice if you have a high risk tolerance and enjoy helping others.

Freelancing

Online freelancing is a career path anyone can choose no matter their skill, experience or situation. A computer and internet connection are the only things you need to begin. You can make money as a freelance writer, graphic designer, sales agent, customer service agent and more. Find freelance sites that connect you with people who need the services you offer, and you will go far. You might think you can't be a freelancer if you lack the required skills. Even if you are not yet an expert, you can take online classes and learn as you go.

MAKE 6 FIGURES WITH TRUCK KING

Continued from page 29

So now you have to manage your life and the life of your driver, because you have to navigate the routes around whatever that individual's situation is. So if they have a graduation coming up, you have to route them home. *Make $250,000 A Year With A Criminal Record And No College Degree* is a real quick read, it's only about 20 pages of literature.

You can actually get everything you need from one page. Everything in the book is supporting information. I will tell you a very brief bio of me. I didn't go into debt because I didn't want to make a book about me, but I wanted to show you that you can relate to me. I was in special education with 5 people in my class, nobody would've thought I'd be where I am today. I was locked up so much as a juvenile before they built the baby bookings, they were building it for me. My brother called me a menace to society. I got kicked out of the state and had to live in New York for an entire year. Everytime I came home to visit I got arrested because I wasn't supposed to be in the state. I dropped out of school. When I was locked up, I used to write to people and they couldn't even read my writing. If you want it, it's nothing that's going to be able to stop you. I have attempted murders on my record. I've been arrested for marijuana, cocaine, and heroin. I got a DUI and a lot of companies frowned upon that. Like I said if you want it bad enough nothing will stop you.

You gotta keep pushing. I had trucks that were repossessed. I took trucks to shops where they ripped me off completely. Either you're going to abandon the truck or scrape up the money and go pick it up. These are the obstacles that you will have to deal with. Drivers get high, they make 2 to 3 thousand a week, get their big check and then quit. DOT chasing them on the highway, people pick up loads and abandon them and then you have to find your truck. It's not easy but it's possible. Also the thing people need to take note about me is that I have documentation to back up everything I've said.

Hood Rich
How to travel for free
And make
$4-500k per year

By Shawn Williamson

@TRUCK_KING85
443-386-6587

It's not one load that I advertised that you can't call me and get a copy of the rate confirmation. I have one truck now and I drive it. People don't understand more trucks doesn't mean more money. You can make more money with one truck, your own authority as a driver with some-one with five trucks that don't drive. We are talking about profit. They may gross more than you, but you can profit more. You think a driver is going to drive all the way to California for you in a Day Cab, no, but in those two weeks I made $32,000. You think I'm going to worry about sleeping in a bed, no. No one will go as hard as you. I go weeks at a time without sleeping in my bed. I have a nice comfortable house, I'm not saying that to brag, I'm telling you that you have to sacrifice.

To the men and women behind enemy lines, this is what you need to do, change your mindset, get a skill and get some experience in that skill, so when you go independent you would be able to properly represent yourself. When you get your money don't spend it on frivolous things, save it, so you can weather the storm.

Why Do Former Inmates Continue To Go Back Inside!

By Ron Stefanski. You can find some of his work in Cultural Daily.

FOR THOSE THAT DON'T KNOW, RECIDIVISM IS WHEN A FORMER CRIMINAL OFFENDER COMMITS AN ADDITIONAL CRIME AND RETURNS TO INCARCERATION. WITH THAT BEING SAID, EVEN THOUGH IT'S EASY TO DEFINE RECIDIVISM, FIGURING OUT ITS CAUSE IS A MUCH BIGGER PROBLEM. THIS IS ONE OF THE MOST DIFFICULT QUESTIONS TO ANSWER BECAUSE RECIDIVISM ISN'T CAUSED BY JUST ONE FACTOR. IT CAN BE TIED TO A COMBINATION OF PERSONAL, ECONOMICAL, SOCIOLOGICAL, AND LIFESTYLE FACTORS. IN THIS ARTICLE WE'LL EXAMINE WHAT THOSE FACTORS ARE.

Social Interactions While Incarcerated: While incarceration is focused on punishing and rehabilitating prisoners, one of the most detrimental factors to proper rehabilitation can be the social interactions that inmates have while incarcerated. When someone first gets incarcerated, they may have been associated with a limited social circle of amateur criminals, but prison offers a network of career criminals that could further their criminal prowess. If an inmate isn't actively resisting criminal tendencies and trying to rehabilitate themselves, they may learn more about how to become a better criminal and, upon release, return to a life of crime.

Lack of Employment: When someone finally gets released from prison, even if they want to live a normal life and be a productive member of society, their employment options are severely limited. It's estimated that an individual who has a felony on their record reduces the likelihood of getting a call back from employers by 50%. Lack of employment leads to lack of finances, which can cause an individual to act out of desperation and do whatever is necessary to survive, including committing another crime.

Incarceration Doesn't Treat the Problem: While many institutions state that their goal is to treat inmates and rehabilitate them, anecdotal evidence from our community suggests that most inmates don't feel rehabilitation is part of the experience. In addition to the lack of proper rehabilitation, 2 million people every year are added to the jail system that have a mental illness. The National Center of Addiction and Substance Abuse at Columbia University estimates that of all incarcerated individuals with substance abuse.issues, only 11% of those that need treatment actually receive it while incarcerated. Mental illness and rehabilitation need to be the focus in prison, not just punishment for crimes.

Lack of Employment: When someone finally gets released from prison, even if they want to live a normal life and be a productive member of society, their employment options are severely limited. It's estimated that an individual who has a felony on their record reduces the likelihood of getting a call back from employers by 50%. Lack of employment leads to lack of finances, which can cause an individual to act out of desperation and do whatever is necessary to survive, including committing another crime.

Depression and Desperation: With all of the mental health issues in prisons, where certain studies have estimated 31% of females and 14.5% of males have a serious mental issue, without proper treatment these issues will carry over into when the inmate is released. The lack of employment, negative social stigmas, and lack of support upon release can put inmates into a deeper state of depression and lead to desperate attempts to get the things that they want such as drugs to escape their reality.

Being Overwhelmed by Society: For those that have served long sentences in prison, it's not surprising that some inmates are intimidated and overwhelmed upon release. Being incarcerated forces an individual into a rigid schedule and they are required to follow rules every single day. Once they are released, they have much more freedom and this can lead to them feeling overwhelmed and full of anxiety. This feeling may lead to substance abuse to cope with these issues, which can lead to additional crimes. *Continued on page 35*

In Two Years

WE SHOULD BE GETTING CLOSER TO OUR GOAL.WE'RE TAKING IT

Slow &Pacing

FOR NOW.WE ARE STILL OUT HERE THAT'S WHAT'S IMPORTANT.

FINANCIAL PLAYAZ

Continued from page 33

Not Changing Lifestyle/Social Circle Upon Release: Part of a successful rehabilitation is for individuals to distance themselves from negative influences upon release. Unfortunately, this is much easier said than done. Many times, former inmates will go back to the same crowd of people they used to associate with because finding a new group isn't easy to do. Further, if gang activity is involved, it might be very difficult to leave their old group for fear of retribution.

Make legit money on the inside.

ANTHONY DAVIS AKA SUGE

I'm currently incarcerated at Fort Dix. I was sentenced to ten years. That's 120 months and I have been down for almost 8 years.

For starters, to make legit money while incarcerated, you need a team. Team work makes the dream work. Seriously if you don't have a team that's driven and motivated it's not going to work. My mom started a security company called JAT Security which stands for Jemel, Anthony, and Terrell. That's my mother, me and my little brother. My brother and I have 30% and my mother has 40%. I also own a real estate company, a record label (Hip Hop Blvd) a clothing line called Forever Fly (f)eeling (l)ike (y)ourself and I'm also coming out with my own seasoning.

All my projects have family members apart of it. My music label, my brother and I own it. My real estate company, my brother and a cousin of mine help out. I also own a credit repair & investment security company called Investment Solutions, where I have 2 of my female cousins working for me as well.

I've wanted to make my own seasoning because I love to cook. I just never put the time in to sit and go over things, but when you're locked up you have all the time in the world to put shit together and to really think about life.

Support goes a long way and I do shit from the heart. My boy Rain sent me a letter saying he was home, so I told my brother to send him a band and told him to take care of his business.

Being legit is a good thing, you always need a foundation that's the importance of it all.

I was legit making beats. I also had a job working for USPS since 2005 until I caught my case in 2013 hustling. This time around I'm going straight legit all the way. The Feds took 10yrs of my life because of a rat who told. I believe in every man taking responsibility for his own actions.

What is credit and why is it important?

A credit score is a number used to provide an overview of your financial health and responsibility. It pulls information from your credit reports and uses an algorithm to come up with a number, somewhere between 300 and 850.

Your credit score carries a lot of weight. The purpose of a credit score and your credit reports is to give lenders and others a quick, easy way to assess the level of risk they will be taking if they enter into a financial relationship with you. It's used by lenders, landlords, insurance companies and others to determine your level of risk and responsibility. So that three digit score tells a lot about you. The higher your credit score, the lower the risk to the lender, because your high credit score indicates you have been financially responsible. Your credit score impacts your ability to purchase a new home or a car or rent an apartment. A good credit score can play into your ability to secure Insurance and can save you lots of money.

Here we'll cover in-depth credit scores, what makes them "good" or "bad" and what you can do to monitor yours!

REACH OUT FOR CREDIT CONSULTATION

One Source Financial Inc., has helped clients work towards fair and accurate credit scores by leveraging their rights. We've helped hundreds of thousands of clients remove unfair, inaccurate and unverified accounts from their credit reports.

HOW IS A CREDIT SCORE GENERATED?

Credit scores are calculated using an algorithm. Anytime you borrow money from a lender, information about that account was likely shared with at least one of the three major credit bureaus (Equifax, TransUnion and Experian). If you're looking for credit from a bank or credit union, they will use the information from these credit bureaus to make a lending decision.

CREDIT SCORE RANGES

There are various different credit scoring formulas currently in use, but most of them operate on a scale of 300–850. Each credit score has its own variations on the same basic concept. The most commonly used scoring method, maintained by the Fair Isaac Corporation, is the Fico Score. If a lender has ever pulled your credit report and gotten back to you with your current credit score, there is a very good chance it was a FICO Score they gave you, as the FICO Score is used in about 90 percent of all lending decisions made in the U.S. Although there are no official distinctions, the following credit score ranges are generally accepted ranges used by many lenders:

1. 300–549 - Bad
2. 550–649 - Poor
3. 650–699 - Fair
4. 700–749 - Good
5. 750–850 – Excellent

To put everything in perspective, the bottom line is the higher your credit score, the more likely you are to be extended credit, and the less you will have to pay for it.

WHAT MAKES A GOOD CREDIT SCORE?

The simplest answer to this question comes from FICO® themselves: "If you pay all your bills on time every time, keep revolving balances low, and only open new credit when necessary, you will have a good FICO® Score. It really is that simple."

If you want to go into it a little deeper in this subject. The following five factors are key to achieving and maintaining a good credit score, no matter which score is being used. The percentages listed refer to how heavily these factors weigh into your FICO® Score:

Payment History: 35%

Lenders want to see that you consistently pay your bills on time, and that you pay at least the minimum required amount each time they're due. Even one late payment or missed payment can have a serious impact on your credit score, so prioritize making payments on time and for the full amount.

Credit Utilization: 30%

This is how much of the total amount of credit available is being used. The rule of thumb is to keep your credit utilization at or below 30% of your overall credit limits. For instance, if you have a total credit limit of $20,000 available, try to keep your balance below $6,000.

Credit Age: 15%

All else being equal, a longer credit history scores better than a shorter one, so the older your card is the better. To raise your score, even if an account has a $0 balance, do not close the account. As it stays on your record, it adds to your total available credit and the total length of your credit history. Do not close any credit card account.

Number of Inquiries: 10%

A hard inquiry occurs when a lender pulls your credit report in response to your request for credit, such as when you apply for a credit card, car or a mortgage loan. A large number of inquiries in a fairly short time will drop your score dramatically, so make sure to do your due diligence ahead of time and only fill out an application when it is truly needed and/or you are certain you can handle the responsibility.

Different Types of Credit: 10%

This factor displays a well-rounded credit history. Primarily, the mix will consist of revolving debt (credit cards) and installment debt (car loans, student loans).

WHAT CAUSES A BAD CREDIT SCORE?

There are several ways to hurt your credit score. I'm sure you have an idea from the things we listed above. Some other common mistakes people make that result in a bad credit score include:

- Making late payments (Payment History)
- Maxing out credit cards (Credit Utilization)
- Applying for too many credit cards (Number of Inquiries)
- Closing $0 balance lines of credit (Credit Age, Credit Utilization)

Continued on next page

- Refusing to use credit at all (Credit Age, Different Type of Credit)

There are more things that can negatively impact your credit. It's important to remember that inaction can have just as much impact as positive or negative action, so it's important to be proactive if you want to improve your credit score.

WHAT ARE THE IMPLICATIONS OF BAD CREDIT?

Bad credit certainly won't do anything in your favor to impress potential lenders, landlords or employers. The bottom line is they are likely to view your unstable financial past as a good indication of your future financial behavior. Because of the perceived business risk, lenders may not approve you.

If they do, they'll likely charge you higher interest rates. Employers may decide to pass you over in favor of someone with better credit. Additionally, insurance companies may charge higher premiums to compensate for your perceived high-risk.

HOW TO IMPROVE YOUR CREDIT SCORE

There are many ways to improve your credit score. Keeping old credit cards open is one way to improve the age of your credit history. Another is to spread out credit card debt across multiple cards. Always pay off your highest interest debt first and make payments before credit card companies report it to the credit bureaus.

Not every individual with a bad credit score is a high risk. Cases of identity theft, inaccurate information and other examples of unfair credit reporting may depict you in an unjustifiably wrong light. It's up to you to determine whether your credit score accurately reflects your financial past. That's why you should take advantage of your rights under the Fair Credit Reporting Act, including your right to a free credit report from each of the major credit bureaus every year, and the right to dispute any, unfair, inaccurate or unsubstantiated items you find on that report.

The good news is that Federal Law regulates credit reporting agencies. You have a right to a fair and accurate credit report and can dispute information that is inaccurate, unfair or unverifiable.

If you're not sure how to dispute information on your credit reports, or feel overwhelmed, you can seek help from qualified professionals who can guide you through the process and act as advocates for you.

One Source Financial Inc., has helped clients work towards fair and accurate credit reports by leveraging their rights. Credit reporting is a complex process, but asking the right questions about your credit report doesn't have to be. Call One Source Financial Inc. at (800) 654-9901 or email onesourcefinancialinc@gmail.com to schedule a personalized credit consultation and see if we can help you repair damaged credit. Do something today that your future self will thank you for!

Call 1-800-654-9901

GOD ALMIGHTY TOUGHEST SOLIDER (G.A.T.S)

Bulletproof Bodies is about perfecting your inner potential and your outer potential, meaning it's just not about bulletproofing your physical appearance but also your health because everyone on social media worry about their appearance and it shouldn't be that way, your health should be first. So when you do that your byproduct is your appearance.

FP: So when did you come up with your brand Bulletproof Bodies?

G: When I was talking to you and seeing you everyday in the mess hall.

FP: So when you were incarcerated you came up with the brand, took your test and got your license?

G: I became an elite trainer, not a personal trainer an elite trainer.

FP: Explain the difference.

G: Elite trainer means I have multiple certifications, that means that I'm not just a
regular personal trainer, I'm certified for strengthening and conditioning, meaning I can train athletes on any level. I'm also certified as a nutritionist, which means I can recommend what to

eat in addition to the regular personal training. I have certifications through the ISA and on my certificate is say's elite trainer.

FP: So you have certifications as a personal trainer and an elite?

G: You can have elite, personal, and master. I'm working on my masters now.

FP: On social media you have a nice amount of clients you train.

G: I have a huge fan base. My clients love me wherever I go. I train clients in the Bronx,
Queens. Right now I'm in Pittsburgh training with Tom Yankello. He was Roy Jones trainer.

FP: So you can go to any gym to train?

G: I can go to any gym in the world to train.

THE SECRET WEAPON

FP: I know a lot of gyms don't let you train unless you work for that gym.

G: Yes, absolutely. What I do as an independent contractor is go to the gym and let them know that I have a team of trainers that will market for them and promote their gym. We will also get the clients to purchase packages and we will take a percentage of it. If the owner agrees, I'll be a contractor for that gym and then I'll bring in my team and plant Bulletproof bodies in that gym.

FP) So you're independent contractor and you work out of many gyms?

G: I do work for a gym called CKO, but I also bring my own clients there and just pay them rent.

FP) Do they need a membership to work out of that gym?

G: No, they come to the gym and I just pay them for that hour.

FP) Do you have any merchant?

G: Yes, I have Bulletproof resistance bands, facemasks and shirts.

FP) I commend you because everything you talked about doing with the boxing, personal trainer, excuse me, elite trainer all the times I saw you walking across the yard with those books are paying dividends now. So let me give you your props.

G: Yeah, yeah, thank you.

FP: So with boxing do you have a fight coming up?

G: They want me to get ready for this Golden Glove tournament in April. I don't know, I haven't really been training, it's been really hard, working on my company and finding a solid trainer. I went to Morris Park in the Bronx training with Aron Davis. *Continued on next page.*

He was a middleweight champion, I was working with him for a few weeks until he got sick and lucky Tom Yankello called me so I could come down to Pittsburgh. He is also busy working with a pro named Willy
Shaw and he's a great fighter. He also has an amateur that's top 5 in the country named Danny, and since I'm the least experienced I get put on the back-burner. I need consistency if I'm going to take it seriously.

FP) So you don't know if you're going to fight in April?

G: Hopefully, I'm training now so lets see what happen.

If you do fight we will be there holding you down and will have the pictures for the readers.

Gats) Well right now I'm in Pittsburgh for a month perfecting my craft, sharpening my tools so I can go into the tournament representing Bulletproof Bodies. All of these clients that I train expect me to go in there to represent.

FP) How did you accumulate all of your clients?

To build up your client base you have to first work at a gym, then once you start training people, clients are going to start gravitating to you and once that happens they're going to start talking about you and that's the best promotion.

FP) What about social media?

G) Social Media is good if you already have that client base and you want to build from there. If you go on social media and you start promoting, and no one ever heard of you, even if you look good, they're not coming to you, especially females and they are the clientele.
Guys spend money with us, but not like women. Females don't want to train with someone they don't know, you might be a pervert, so It's good when you start at the gym and get referrals now you're able to post on your social media page your training clients and then you build your base from there. Think about it this way, it's much easier for you to meet a girl if you were introduced to her by her friend as opposed to walking up to her on the streets, you feel me.

FP) I like the way you put that. Now when you go away for a month don't you lose money and clients?

G: It's definitely hard, I take a huge loss, that's why it's really hard for me, either I'm going to box or do Bulletproof Bodies and doing both is extremely hard,

that's why there is no momentum in either. Right now me being in Pittsburgh for a month, I dropped Bulletproof Bodies. Only thing that's making money while I'm away, is the merchant other than that I'm not making any money. That's why I have been promoting a lot of online training because I can't be there. Since the pandemic, online training has become big, so that's another lane to
get money.

FP: So how's that working out for you?

G: I have a few clients, working on more before I start. Once I have 10 I will get started. I'm going to keep working hard and it's all going to come together Interview me next year
and you will see the progress.

FP: So what's more important to you, becoming a world champion or Bulletproof Bodies?

G: I always wanted to become a world champion since I was 19, becoming a world champion will help me finance Bulletproof Bodies. I feel that the money I make from becoming a world champion will help Bulletproof Bodies get to where it needs to be. I have to get the finance from somewhere, me just training individual clients is not real money, it's enough for me to pay bills and get buy. Someway somehow, I have to find a way to finance my company and I figure boxing will be the best way to do it. Hopefully I can do it through boxing, if not I have to find another way to fuel my business. I have a vision, I'm my biggest investor, I tell people my vision, I don't know if they believe in it, but I do.

FP) We will build, because there are a lot of different ways to get capital that you can tap into and I'm going to help you anyway that I can. Give a shout out to the men and women behind the wall?

"Never let your memories be greater than your dreams."

Learn how to live off of $30,000 a year!!

Content provided by National Debt Relief

Do you believe you just couldn't live on $30,000 a year? Well, you could. For that matter, many families do. In some cases it's because that's how much they earn after taxes. In others it's because they choose to live on that $30,000 so they can save the rest for retirement to buy a house or pay for their children's college education.

You would need to earn a bit more

To have a net income of $30,000 a year means that the only federal tax you would be paying would be your FICO (Federal Insurance Compensations Act) tax, which is currently at 6.2% This means your total annual gross pay would have to be at least $31,860 or $2650 a month or $15.30 an hour.

A typical budget

What would your budget look like if you were living on $30,000 a year? Here are the five major categories and the percentages you could budget for each.

Mortgage or rent

The maximum percentage you should spend on housing is 25% to 30% of your income. This should include your utilities and other monthly home expenses such as homeowners or renters insurance.

This means to live on $30,000 a year you would spend no more than $625 to $750 a month for housing.

Transportation

You should spend about 18% of your income on transportation whether you drive, take the bus, train or Uber. If you drive, this needs to include your gas, tolls, car payments (if applicable) and your auto insurance. This means you will need to budget about $450 for transportation.

Savings

Even when living on $30,000 a year, it's essential that you save at least 10% of your income. This would be approximately $200 per month. This will add up so that by the end of the year you would have a nice $3000 cushion.

Food

You will need to spend no more than 15% of your budget for food. This means about $400 a month. If you have a large family, this just might be difficult but it is what you should shoot for.

Internet/telephone

It's best to keep your spending on the Internet and your phone (including cell phones) at no more than $170 a month or about 6% of your total budget.

The biggest drain

Without question the biggest drain on any budget is the cost of housing. If your mortgage or rent exceeds $750, you may have to find a cheaper place to live or find a roommate. You maybe able to lower your mortgage by refinancing.

The interest rates on mortgages today are at almost an all time low. As an example of this, www.bestrateloans.com is currently advertising a 30-year fixed rate mortgage with an interest rate of 4.125% and the website www.bankrate.com reports that the average interest (as of this writing) for a 30-year fixed rate mortgage is 4.33% (4.39 APR).

Everything else

What this would leave is $680 for everything else. And since everything else could be a lot of things you will need to get creative or to put this another way, you will need to live on the cheap. You could save money on food by going to the grocery store and comparison shop for your auto insurance to make sure you're getting the best deal possible. And if you're carrying more than $200 a month in debt, you need to find ways to get rid of it.

One of the best methods we've found is to "snowball" your debts. This means ordering them from the one with the highest interest rate down to the one with the lowest. Then focus everything on paying off the debt with the highest interest rate as this will free up the maximum amount of money you would then use to pay off the one with the second highest interest rate and so on. While you're doing this be sure to keep making the minimum payments on your other debts. Follow this strategy and you could be completely debt-free in just a year or two – depending on how much you owe.

Other ways to trim costs

In addition to the tips given above there are some other ways that you could cut costs to stay within that $30,000. Here are six of them:

Become an extreme couponer

We have seen cases where people have cut their food bill from $800 a month to less than $400 by extreme couponing. There are websites where you can get manufacturers' coupons that you can use at almost any store. You can even buy coupons in bulk. Virtually every grocery chain now has loyalty programs where you automatically receive good money-saving coupons at least once a month. The store we use emails us 18 pages of money-saving offers each month. We just choose the ones we want and they are then downloaded onto our loyalty card.

Eat out but sensibly

There is absolutely no reason to pay full price for meals when you dine out. You can get cheap gift cards from Restaurants.com that'll save you 50% or more. So when you go out to eat, this could cut a $60 bill down to $30 and save you as much as $1440 a year.

Get your entertainment flicks for less

Going to the movies can cost at least $30 and that's without popcorn. Find a theater rewards program to earn free tickets and snacks. You could pay for your family fun using your cash back debit card. Or you could stream movies and TV shows using Netflix for just $8.99 a month or if you really want to go the cheap route there is RedBox where a relatively new movie costs just $1.50 a night.

Ditch that second car

If you have two cars in one household, seriously consider ditching one of them. That would basically cut your transportation costs in half. You would save even more if you have a loan on that car as you could sell it and pay off the loan. That would cut both your debt and your transportation costs.

Save on clothing

The first thing you can do to cut your clothing costs is to stop buying clothes that you can't afford. Don't try to keep up with Jones, move at your own pace. You could save a lot of cash by shopping at discount stores such as T.J. Maxx and Marshalls. And consignment stores can be a good way to get designer-label clothing that's been gently used – for far less than if you were to buy it new. Remember it's not about your clothes, it's about your bank account and sticking to your plan.

Save money with your smartphone

There are a number of apps available for use on Android or iPhones that could help you save money. One that we like is RedLaser. It's available for use on the iPhone, Windows phone 7 and Android phones. The way it works is you simply take a photo of a product's barcode. RedLaser will then search, compare and spit out a list of the best available prices for all online and brick-and-mortar stores within the radius of a few miles. When you find the lowest price for an item, you can use "By It Now" directly through the app.

A second helpful app is Slice, which can be used on the iPhone or Android phones. It syncs with your Yahoo or Gmail accounts and when it's opened will immediately go hunting in your inbox and automatically keep track of your shipped orders then alert you as to price drops that could help you take advantage of adjustments at merchants that offer this. Walmart, Kohl's and Target are examples of adjustment-happy merchants.

A third of these useful apps is Retail Me Not. It's only available for use on the iPhone. What it does is give you access to literally tens of thousands of coupons and deals from retailers that are convenient to you. This enables you to do your shopping online directly from your phone and even redeem coupons directly in the store from the app.

Coupon Sherpa can also help you save money. Plus it eliminates the need to clip, organize and store coupons. It's website offers both printable and mobile coupons. You can tell the app your favorite stores to easily track their latest coupons.

Finally, there is the app Key Ring. It's free and can be used on an Android, iPhone, iPad or Blackberry. What it does is give you the ability to store all of your loyalty cards. All you have to do is take a picture of the ID number for each card and it will be stored in the app. Then your loyalty cards will be available to use whenever you need them and you will never leave any savings behind.

TRADELINES

BY ONE SOURCE FINANCIAL

One question we often hear in the tradeline industry is "Do tradelines still work in 2021?" Fortunately, we can say with certainty that tradelines do still work in 2021, and we are confident they will continue to be effective for years to come. To explain our answer, we will delve into the history of authorized user tradelines and the policies that regulate the tradeline industry.

WHY DO TRADELINES WORK?

Although the term "tradeline" could refer to any account in your credit file, usually in our industry people use the word as shorthand for authorized user tradelines, or accounts on which you are an authorized user.

Credit card companies allow cardholders to add authorized users (AUs) to their accounts, which are people who are authorized to use the account but are not liable for any charges incurred. For example, a business owner could add an employee as an AU of their credit card, or a parent could add their child.

When someone is added as an AU, often the full history of the account is shown in the credit reports of both the primary user and the AU, regardless of when the AU was added to the account. Therefore, the AU may have years of credit history associated with the account reflected in their file as soon as they are added.

This is why obtaining an AU tradeline through a family member or friend is a common way for people to start establishing a credit history. In fact, studies estimate that 20%-30% of Americans have at least one AU account.

Why are authorized users able to share the benefits of the primary user's credit rating, even though they are not liable for the debt? This policy is a result of the Equal Credit Opportunity Act of 1974 (ECOA).

Before ECOA was passed, creditors would often report accounts shared by married couples as being only in the husband's name. This prevented women from building up a credit history and credit score rating in their own names, which in turn prevented them from being able to obtain credit independent of their husbands.

In response to this unequal treatment, ECOA was passed to prohibit discrimination in lending. The federal law made it illegal for creditors to discriminate on the basis of sex, marital status, race, color, religion, national origin, age, or receipt of public assistance.
This means that creditors may not consider this information when deciding whether or not to grant credit to an applicant or determining the terms of the credit.

Regulation B is a section of ECOA that specifically requires that creditors report spousal AU accounts to the credit bureaus and consider them when lenders evaluate a consumer's credit history.

Generally, creditors do not distinguish between AUs that are spouses and those that are not when reporting to the credit bureaus, which effectively requires the credit bureaus to treat all AU accounts in the same way.

As a result of this policy, the practice of "piggy backing credit" emerged as a common and acceptable way for individuals with good credit to help their spouses, children, and loved ones build credit or improve their credit. The practice of piggybacking is the foundation of

the tradeline industry. In a piggybacking arrangement, a consumer pays a fee to "rent" an authorized user position on someone else's tradeline. The age and payment history of that tradeline then show up on the consumer's credit report as an authorized user account.

ECOA was passed in large part to prevent creditors from discriminating against women and to provide equal credit opportunities to women.

ARE TRADELINES LEGAL?

It is understandable that there is some confusion about this since not many people are aware of the idea of tradelines for sale, although the practice has been in use for decades.

While One Source Financial Inc., cannot provide legal advice, we can refer to several official sources, including the Federal Trade Commission, who have indicated that it is legal to buy and sell tradelines

While tradelines are not illegal, historically, they have not been accessible to everyone. The high cost of tradelines meant that only the wealthy could afford to purchase tradelines for credit piggybacking. Today, however, innovations in the industry have lowered the cost of tradelines, making them affordable to a much wider audience.

One Source Financial Inc., is proud to be leading the tradeline industry in automating the process of buying and selling tradelines, offering some of the lowest tradeline prices in the industry, educating consumers on the credit system, and making tradelines accessible to everyone.

Our goal is to provide equal opportunities to those who do not have access to authorized user tradelines through friends and family by providing an online platform that allows for a greater network of connections.

BUT DIDN'T CREDIT CARD PIGGYBACKING GET BANNED?

Fair Isaac Corporation (FICO), the creator of the widely used FICO credit score, did try to change its scoring model to eliminate the benefits of authorized user tradelines, although they were ultimately unsuccessful. The firm announced that they were planning to devise a way to allow "real" AUs to keep the benefits of their AU tradelines while at the same time discounting the value of AU tradelines for consumers who FICO deemed to be "gaming the system."

FICO admitted to Congress that they could not legally discriminate between AUs based on marital status due to ECOA. While this statement understandably caused a lot of concern among consumers of tradelines, as it turns out, FICO was never able to implement this change in their scoring system.

At a congressional hearing in 2008, Fair Isaac's president admitted that they could not legally distinguish between spousal AUs and other users, because discriminating based on marital status would unlawfully violate ECOA.

After consulting with Congress and multiple federal agencies, FICO was blocked from discriminating against AU account holders. Consequently, all AU accounts are still being considered in FICO 8, the most widely used credit scoring model.

FICO admitted to Congress that they could not legally discriminate between AUs based on marital status due to ECOA.

In addition, studies have shown that accounting for AU data helps make credit scoring models more accurate, so it is actually in FICO's best interest to continue including all AU accounts in their credit scoring models.

In working with thousands of consumers over the years, our results prove that in 2021, AU tradelines still remain an effective way to add information to an individual's credit report, regardless of the relationship between the primary user and the authorized user.

Here's another piece of evidence that proves that authorized user tradelines still work in 2021: many banks actually promote the practice of becoming an

authorized user for the specific purpose of boosting one's credit score. To see this for yourself, all you need to do is go to any major bank's website and search for "authorized user." You are almost guaranteed to see several articles pop up that talk about becoming an authorized user in order to build a credit history.

HOW DO WE KNOW TRADELINES WILL CONTINUE TO WORK IN THE FUTURE?

Given that FICO has already targeted the tradeline industry before, it makes sense to wonder whether tradelines will still work in the years to come if FICO eventually does succeed in coming up with a way to discriminate against certain AUs.

Thankfully, we can rest assured in knowing that the tradeline business will be around for a long time. The reason that we can be sure of this is that the credit industry is extremely slow to adapt, so even if FICO were to roll out a new credit score model that can tell which AUs purchased their tradelines, it would take years, if not decades, for this new credit score to be adopted across the entire financial industry. Let us explain why this is the case.

Credit scoring is a complicated process, and all lenders have their own guidelines when it comes to underwriting. FICO has many different scoring models, and the specific versions used to evaluate credit applicants vary widely between industries and even

between individual lenders within the same industry.

Currently, the three major credit bureaus (Equifax, Experian, and TransUnion) use the version called FICO 8, which debuted in 2008. Consequently, this is also the version that most lenders use for measuring consumer risk for various types of credit, such as personal loans, student loans, and retail credit cards.

Most widely used credit scoring models still include authorized user "piggybacking" accounts.

However, according to FICO, the mortgage industry still relies on the much older FICO score models 2, 4, and 5. Auto lenders sometimes use FICO 8, while many still use FICO 2, 4, and 5. Credit card companies may use versions 2, 3, 4, 5, and 8.

As if this isn't complicated enough, many lenders also use proprietary credit-scoring guidelines specific to their businesses. According to FICO's website, "It is up to each lender to determine which credit score they will use and what other financial information they will consider in their credit review process."

As you can see from the wide range of versions used, lenders are extremely slow to adapt to changes in FICO's credit scoring model. In addition, their underwriting processes have been built around previous versions of FICO.

All of the credit score data they have accumulated over time is only accurate for the particular version that was used to calculate it.

Transitioning to a completely new credit score model would require businesses to expend significant resources on updating their technological systems, collecting and analyzing new consumer data, training employees, and possibly incurring financial losses as a consequence of not being able to rely on the consumer data they collected while using older credit score models.

For these reasons, most lenders tend to be very reluctant to introduce the latest FICO credit scoring model.

Lenders use credit scoring models that are specific to their industries, so they tend to resist changing to newer models. Photo by Investment Zen

For these reasons, most lenders tend to be very reluctant to introduce the latest FICO credit scoring model.

So, even if FICO were to successfully eliminate authorized user data in future credit scoring models, it is likely that it would take years or even decades for lenders to adapt to this change.

In addition, as the 2008 congressional hearing showed, FICO will face pushback from the federal government if they try to

eliminate authorized user benefits again. It is highly unlikely that a large company like FICO would want to risk being shut down by the federal government for violating the law

Consumers wouldn't stand for it, either. In the Washington post, J.W. Elphinstone wrote, "Other consumers besides credit renters stand to lose with the change, namely those for whom authorized user accounts were designed… there's no way to distinguish these from the latest crop of strangers trying to augment their scores. Lenders who want to find out more information about others on credit card accounts are hindered by the Fair Credit Reporting Act and privacy laws."

FINAL THOUGHTS

When FICO took the issue of piggybacking all the way up to Congress in 2008, they made headlines in their fight against the practice.

This was also during the same time that the subprime mortgage meltdown began which preceded the Great Recession. The entire mortgage industry had to be overhauled and many people assumed that the tradeline industry went down along with it.

What did not make headlines is that FICO's push to do away with the authorized user tradeline industry actually failed due to the government upholding ECOA and the FTC affirming that the practice of buying and selling tradelines is allowed.

The banks themselves even promote credit card piggybacking

among friends, family, and co-workers.

Now, in 2021, this option is more affordable and accessible than ever through companies such as One Source Financial Inc, who help provide equal credit opportunity for all by making it possible for nearly anyone to buy tradelines.

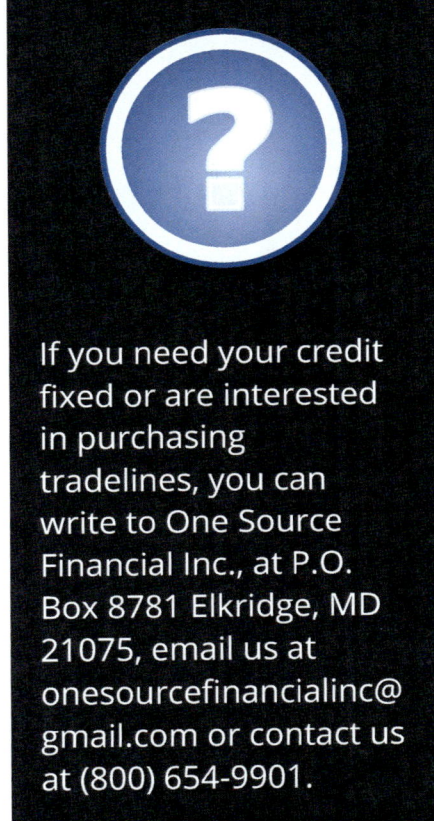

If you need your credit fixed or are interested in purchasing tradelines, you can write to One Source Financial Inc., at P.O. Box 8781 Elkridge, MD 21075, email us at onesourcefinancialinc@gmail.com or contact us at (800) 654-9901.

If you have something positive going on and you want to share it with the Financial Playaz or if there is something that you want to learn or know about you can write to us at P.O. Box 8781 Elkridge, MD 21075.

WHO HAS THE MOST
money in the rap game?

The hip hop industry is a world of its own with different talents and styles and it also gives room for new rappers to explore and to become better rappers. At the same time, hip hop is a grieving industry and there are rappers from almost all parts of the world earning and becoming better each day. Here are the top rappers with cool money in the industry: Nicki Minaj, Timbaland, Pitbull, Mike Diamond, Ad-Rock, Swizz Beatz, Birdman, LL Cool J,Pharrell Williams, Snoop Dogg, Lil Wayne, Ice Cube, Usher, Drake, Master P, Eminem, Dr. Dre, P. Diddy, Jay-Z, Kanye West, Wiz Khalifa, J. Cole.

TOP 10 HIGHEST PAID RAPPERS IN 2021

Kanye Omari West is from Chicago, IL. West is a rapper, producer, fashion designer and businessman. He has a net worth of 1.8 billion.

Shawn Corey Carter aka Jay Z was born in New York, and he is a rapper, songwriter, record executive, businessman, and media proprietor. He has a net worth over $1 billion.

Sean Love Combs aka Puffy, or Diddy, is an American rapper, record producer, record executive, and entrepreneur. Diddy has a net worth of $895 million.

Andre Romelle Young Aka Dr Dre is from Compton, California, United States. It is said that Dr. Dre earned about $620 million in one year alone from his music career. Dr. Dre's net worth is $865 million.

Percy Robert Miller also known as Master P, is from New Orleans, LA. Master P is a rapper, actor, record producer, entrepreneur, and former basketball player. Master P's estimated net worth is $245 million.

Marshall Bruce Mathers III aka Eminem is from Saint Joseph, MO. Eminem has been very successful in the hip-hop industry with a solid bank account.His net worth is estimated to be $220 million.

TOP 10 HIGHEST PAID RAPPERS IN 2021

Aubrey Drake Graham, popularly known as Drake is from Toronto, Canada. Drake is an ambassador for the NBA's Toronto Raptors, and has succeeded the real estate portfolio. Drake has a net worth of $190 million.

Dwayne Michael Carter Jr also known as Lil Wayne is from New Orleans, LA. Lil Wayne became popular after his debut album 'Tha block is hot'. Wayne is also an author and an entrepreneur. His net worth is estimated to be $158 million.

Pharrell Lanscilo Williams is an singer, songwriter, record producer, fashion designer, and entrepreneur. He owns his own record label and textile company Bionic Yarn. Pharrell Williams has a net worth of $200 million.

Calvin Cordozar Broadus Jr., also known as Snoop Dogg, is a rapper, singer, songwriter, actor, media personality, and businessman. He has more than $152 million in net worth.

Conclusion

Rappers are a great means of entertainment to the world, they deliver the best and also pass meaningful messages.

Most of these top rappers didn't just get their money from sales of albums alone, they try to invest in almost every kind of production they could.

This article highlights the best and top highest paid rappers in the world.

WHY MOST RAPPERS ARE BROKE?

I saw a video on this and I wanted to make my own version. I have actually bought jewelry and I know rappers who have spent half a million on jewelry too and didn't end up as broke rappers. This is a Smart Rapper. I'm not the guy that goes out and tells you to spend $50,000 on jewelry. I'm the guy that tells you how to maximize $1,000 for your rap career so you don't go broke as a rapper. In this article, I let you know how I got my chain and WHY I got my chain, as well as the benefits of it and why I will never be like these other broke rappers. I made the right decisions with my money, and I want to help you make the right decisions with your money and rap career too.

WHERE BROKE RAPPERS START GETTING POOR?

First, let's talk about what happens when YOU start making a lot of money as an artist. You'll start making so much money, it'll be 100 times more money than you were ever making before.

Since you were so used to being poor and not having any money to spend, you can suddenly spend money. As you start spending money, spending becomes a habit, you move from fearing a $10 lunch to spending $20 per meal then $30 per meal then $50 per meal.

TRUST ME This happened to me when I was a broke rapper. I used to be afraid to spend $7 on lunch and think Chick-Fil-A was expensive. You suddenly feel FREE spending money and start spending it on anything and
everything you want. This is where the problem arises for broke rappers. This is how rappers have gone broke, and how people like Mike Tyson go from being worth $400 MILLION dollars to going bankrupt. You probably think, "How can you possibly spend 400 MILLION DOLLARS! You probably could buy everything you ever wanted and it wouldn't cost more than 5 million and that's including cars, houses, AND jewelry." You're only supposed to buy what you can afford, but people lose track of what they can afford.

How I Prevent This From Happening?

You know I am here to inspire you, so this article is to prepare you for when you get rich and help you understand WHEN you can go buy a chain. You probably want a chain right now. You want a nice car, you want the best outfits, you want all that stuff, but do you have a solid home studio? Do you have your microphone and preamp so your art can shine? Realistically, your music is what is going to make you the money, right? If you are investing more money into things that don't make you money, how are you going to grow your career and make MORE money?

The way to NOT go broke is to invest in everything you NEED first, so you can create the stuff that will make you money. Then you can start buying your toys. Let me tell you what I did when I was a broke rapper. I started making serious money and the first thing I did WAS buy my studio equipment, then I bought a new camera to increase the video quality for you guys to enjoy my videos more so you take me more seriously, then I bought and furnished my Smart Rapper show set so you take me more seriously as well. THEN, I went and got the car. I saved for 8 months and had a lot of back up money. I paid my taxes, THEN I went and bought my chain.

Everything I have mentioned that I bought is completely tax-writable. Meaning I don't have to pay the taxes on that money spent. Why? Because it was all to further my business so I wouldn't end up like all the broke rappers.

Broke Rappers Buy Jewelry

Now let's talk about the chain.

The chain is my logo. It's almost 600 stones, SI1s and VS Stones. White Gold custom made. It cost me around $10,000, but I wear it and since it's my logo, it's marketing. Since I need it for my image, it's tax-writable.

Note, I didn't just go buy this chain immediately. I saved up for over a year and had a lot of back up money before I got it.

I also bought a fake one to see how I would feel wearing a chain with my name on it. I tested it, I loved it, and then I invested in the chain.

Most rappers go and just buy random chains, watches, and rings just to glisten. What a waste of money! $60,000 watch? What the hell!? And that watch doesn't market them. It's just useless jewelry to shine and worry about getting stolen. Smart Rappers don't spend money they don't have. What good are 8 chains worth $50,000 each when you suddenly can't make your car payment? That's flat out stupid.

> "Be a Smart Rapper so you don't end up like these broke rappers."

In an Conclusion

If you get jewelry, make sure you can truly afford it. Keep track of how much money you make. Invest in what you need first so you can always create more in order to make money back. Business first then toys. Rappers go broke because they aren't SMART. They let their emotions of, "I NEED THIS NOW," get in the way of their long term goals.

The last thing you want to happen to you is that your career starts taking off, but you spend $30,000 on some jewelry, and somehow you didn't get a check you expected. Now you don't have marketing dollars or the money to shoot the next music video for your new single. Now your career is at a standstill until you get more money. You'd feel like quite a dumb rapper.

THE BEST WAYS TO BECOME A MILLIONAIRE

BY DANA ANSPACH

You can find her best work in the Balance

Think you can't become a millionaire? You might be surprised at the ways you can get there. But before you get too excited, if you think becoming a millionaire means fancy cars, a lavish house, and an upscale lifestyle, think again. If you had a million and spent it that way, you'd blow through it pretty quickly. In retirement, $1 million might provide you an income of $50,000 a year. You'd need to invest it using either withdrawal-rate rules or a time-segmented approach. However, having a million dollars' worth of assets is a fine goal, and it may be easier than you think. Here are six ways to become a millionaire:

1. Develop your career and expertise

Consider the old-fashioned approach: Work hard to build skills, make yourself valuable, and you might receive more when you apply yourself in a career. Many millionaires have made it because they have worked hard and found a way to earn a lot of money. They may have earned degrees and professional certifications to increase their knowledge. They may have been willing to spend time doing low-paid internships and apprenticeships to learn their crafts. As they have gained greater expertise and stronger footholds in their fields, they have begun to earn more.

Food For Thought: Not every work investment guarantees a certain level of income, and not all career paths are straight lines. Skill-building, work experience, and self-betterment are surefire ways to enhance your value in the workplace.

2. Create a side hustle

Income is only one end of the millionaire equation. However, it's a crucial one. The more you earn, the more you can put away toward your million dollar goal. If you have a great job with plenty of surplus income, you're on your way. If not, you may need to get creative. A side hustle can be a smart way to augment your current income and could become quite fruitful on its own.

Create intellectual property

Intellectual property includes products of unique creativity, such as books, patented inventions, songs, scripts, trademarked products, and art. There are many ways to make your projects profitable, depending on your craft and industry.

- Professors use their expertise to write books and consult in their fields.
- Subject-matter experts can design seminars, workshops, and training programs. They sell their books and other materials to make additional income.
- Actors, singers, and musicians create performance art. Many turn themselves and their "image" into a marketable item.
- Writers, painters, and sculptors produce familiar forms of art for sale. They may also expand the scope of their intellectual property to include products or branding for other companies.
- Electricians, plumbers, woodworkers, masons, and other craftspeople may create new tools to use in their industries.
- Medical practitioners, such as surgeons and dentists, may design improved instruments or create patentable medical processes.
- Software developers turn their ideas and code into intellectual property.

When you master your field, find a way to market and sell your services. If you create a new product or service, do the same. You could create subscriptions, licenses, or franchises to expand on your standing in your industry.

Build a business

Creating a new business from scratch is a bold side hustle, because it requires a great deal of time and money upfront. The upside is that you'll have control over the progress, and you'll make more money if it's successful.

If you are in a service business, creating a business model that others can duplicate is challenging; the business is in your area of expertise, and you are the business. You have to figure out a way to train others to do what you do so that you can work on your business rather than work in your business. If you make a product, the challenge is greater; you have to figure out how to market, manufacture, and distribute that product and create a profit.

3. Save diligently, Invest wisely

You can become wealthy by spending less than you make, saving diligently, and investing smartly. How much you need to save depends on how much time you have and the rate of return you will earn.

The biggest mistake that people make that keeps them from making a million is they up-size their lifestyle when their income rises. When your income goes up, the first thing you should increase is the amount you put into your savings.

Food For Thought: Have an emergency fund available so that you don't have to dip into savings for unexpected expenses. Medical bills, home repairs, job loss, natural disasters, and other surprises can be costly. You can salvage or protect your savings by having a financial cushion set aside just for emergencies.

What's more, have a focused plan for how much you'll save every paycheck. If you can put those savings in an account you never touch, you'll be on your way to building that nest egg. (Bonus points if you can put them in an account with a high-interest rate.)

4. Make smart investments

Being a smart investor doesn't always mean playing the stock market and hoping you get in on the next Apple or Amazon. Spend some time learning about the market, and figure out which investments work for you. Think about your budget, how much you can afford to invest, and how comfortable you are with risk.

For one person, this might mean maxing out your 401(k) contributions; another might choose to make robust monthly contributions to an aggressive-leaning investment portfolio; another might choose a simple money market account or CD to get started.

The idea is to avoid having all of your savings in passive accounts. Money that works for you earns steady interest or pays yearly dividends.

Hire a financial professional

You don't need a large amount of extra income to invest. You should only use an amount you're comfortable with. If you are unsure of how to gauge your risk tolerance, a financial advisor can help you learn and build confidence.

Wealth advisors can help you create a road map for your savings goals, point you toward wise investments, and identify areas where you can reduce expenses or get better returns on your investments.

Food For Thought: Even if you're a savvy investor, you may benefit from hiring a professional. Some people even prefer to have someone else research smart investments and do the work for them.

5. Invest in Real Estate

Real estate millionaires put in a lot of hard work early on, but it pays off later in the form of residual rental income, not to mention rising real estate values over time. Those who develop real estate projects also take on significant risks; some pay off big, while others create losses.

Be prepared for ups and downs with your real estate ventures. You'll need to feed money into improvements and maintenance unless you invest in real estate funds that don't require actual property ownership.

6. Create a financial plan

Whether you hire a financial advisor or decide to go solo, you need a plan of action. How much will you save? Where will you invest, and when? Are your current earnings, saving, spending, and investing practices flexible?

What if you get laid off from your job, or you have a financial setback? What if your family grows? Try to prepare for as many outcomes as possible. You don't always have to imagine the the worst-case scenario, but you should know what you'll do if you get off track.

It's also important to keep a balance between your short- and long-term goals. Hitting the million-dollar mark is something that many aspire to. It requires smarts and sacrifices to get there. However, don't forget to tend to your short-term goals and keep a balanced lifestyle along the way.

THE RESPONSIBILITY IS TO KEEP PUSHING IT FORWARD, AND NOT RELYING ON THE SAME OLD GIMMICKS. YOU HAVE TO PUSH IT FORWARD.

Shawn "Jay-Z" Carter

FINANCIAL PLAYAZ

Magazine

—

NEXT ISSUE APRIL 2022   QUARTERLY MAGAZINE

Interested in spotlighting your brand or business in the next issue of our magazine, you can write to One Source Financial Inc., at P.O. Box 8781 Elkridge, MD 21075, email us at onesourcefinancialinc@gmail.com or contact us at (800) 654-9901.

YOUR AD HERE

FINANCE   BUSINESS   ECONOMICS   CREDIT   INSPIRATION

SAVE $19.95 AN ISSUE
OFF COVER PRICE

JUST $15 AN ISSUE!

SUBSCRIBE NOW!

PRINT + DIGITAL ACCESS

FREE GIFT!

FINANCIAL PLAYAZ CLUB

- ✓ one year of digital and print editions
- ✓ receive invitation to VIP ONLY membership
- ✓ access to exclusive content, articles, features, and more...

☐ **YES!**
One year (4 editions) just for $60
**$5 shipping and handling

☐ **8 editions for $120**
FREE SHIPPING

NAME

ADDRESS

CITY   STATE   ZIP CODE

INMATE NUMBER   *Send 'VIP' to onesourcefinancialinc@gmail.com to receive an exclusive invitation to Financial Playaz Club*

SEND MONEY TO ONE SOURCE FINANCIAL INC. P.O. BOX 8781, Elkridge, MD, 21075

**Offer valid in the US only. First issue ships within 6 weeks. Sales maybe added where applicable.

SAVE $19.95 AN ISSUE
OFF COVER PRICE

JUST $15 AN ISSUE!

SUBSCRIBE NOW!

PRINT + DIGITAL ACCESS

FREE GIFT!

FINANCIAL PLAYAZ CLUB

- ✓ one year of digital and print editions
- ✓ receive invitation to VIP ONLY membership
- ✓ access to exclusive content, articles, features, and more...

☐ **YES!**
One year (4 editions) just for $60
**$5 shipping and handling

☐ **8 editions for $120**
FREE SHIPPING

NAME

ADDRESS

CITY   STATE   ZIP CODE

INMATE NUMBER   *Send 'VIP' to onesourcefinancialinc@gmail.com to receive an exclusive invitation to Financial Playaz Club*

SEND MONEY TO ONE SOURCE FINANCIAL INC. P.O. BOX 8781, Elkridge, MD, 21075

**Offer valid in the US only. First issue ships within 6 weeks. Sales maybe added where applicable.